14–18
A NEW VISION
FOR SECONDARY
EDUCATION

ALSO AVAILABLE FROM BLOOMSBURY

Education Policy, Practice and the Professional,
Jane Bates, Sue Lewis and Andy Pickard

Lost Generation?: New Strategies for Youth and Education,
Patrick Ainley and Martin Allen

A Manifesto for the Public University, edited by John Holmwood

*Overschooled but Undereducated: How the Crisis in Education
Is Jeopardizing Our Adolescents*, John Abbott

Wasted: Why Education Isn't Educating, Frank Furedi

14–18
A NEW VISION
FOR SECONDARY
EDUCATION

KENNETH BAKER

**with Mike Tomlinson, Alan Smithers,
Robert B. Schwartz, Andrew Halls,
David Brandon-Bravo, David Harbourne
and Nigel Wyatt**

B L O O M S B U R Y
LONDON • NEW DELHI • NEW YORK • SYDNEY

Bloomsbury Academic

An imprint of Bloomsbury Publishing Plc

50 Bedford Square	175 Fifth Avenue
London	New York
WC1B 3DP	NY 10010
UK	USA

www.bloomsbury.com

First published 2013

British Library Cataloguing-in-Publication Data

A catalogue record for this book is available from the British Library.

ISBN: PB: 978-1-7809-3844-8
HB: 978-1-7809-3739-7
ePub: 978-1-7809-3796-0
PDF: 978-1-7809-3615-4

Library of Congress Cataloging-in-Publication Data

14—18 : a new vision for secondary education / Kenneth Baker; with Mike Tomlinson,
Alan Smithers, Robert B. Schwartz, Andrew Halls, David Brandon-Bravo,
David Harbourne and Nigel Wyatt.
p. cm.
Transforming 14–18 education / Kenneth Baker – A new vision for education in England /
Kenneth Baker – The 14–18 pathways / Kenneth Baker – The qualifications / Mike Tomlinson –
Making 14–18 education a reality / Alan Smithers – Pathways, not tracks: an American
perspective / Robert B. Schwartz – Tiers are not enough: an independent school
perspective / Andrew Halls – Education on a human scale: a middle school perspective /
David Brandon-Bravo – Learning from others / David Harbourne.
Includes bibliographical references and index.
ISBN 978-1-7809-3844-8 (pbk.) – ISBN 978-1-7809-3739-7 (hardcover) –
ISBN 978-1-78093-796-0 (ebook) – ISBN 978-1-78093-615-4 (ebook)
1. Education, Secondary–Great Britain. I. Baker, Kenneth, 1934- editor of compilation.
II. Baker, Kenneth, 1934- Transforming 14–18 education. III. Title. IV. Title: Fourteen Eighteen.
LA635.A465 2013
373.41–dc23
2012042327

Typeset by Newgen Imaging Systems Pvt Ltd, Chennai, India
Printed and bound in Great Britain

Dedicated to the late **Ron Dearing** and

my colleagues at the Baker Dearing Educational Trust

CONTENTS

Preface   ix
Notes on contributors   xii
List of abbreviations   xv

1 Transforming 14–18 education *Kenneth Baker*   1

2 A new vision for education in England
       Kenneth Baker   15

3 The 14–18 pathways *Kenneth Baker*   27

4 The qualifications *Mike Tomlinson*   43

5 Making 14–18 education a reality
       Alan Smithers   57

6 Pathways, not tracks: an American perspective
       Robert B. Schwartz   71

7 Structure and the individual: an independent
       school perspective *Andrew Halls*   85

8 Education on a human scale: a middle school
       perspective *David Brandon-Bravo*   97

9 Learning from others *David Harbourne*   105

Summary of Recommendations   115

Appendix 1: Technical secondary education in England: a brief history *David Harbourne*   119

Appendix 2: The history and strengths of English middle schools *Nigel Wyatt*   141

Glossary   149
References   153
Index   161

PREFACE

Kenneth Baker

Contributors to this book believe that secondary education in England is failing to keep pace with developments in other countries. A fundamental change is needed to prepare young people in our country for adult life and the jobs which our economy will offer in future. Everyone will require a high level of education in the basic subjects and practical skills, leading to further and higher education, apprenticeships and employment. We urgently need a 14–18 curriculum which students find challenging and relevant to their personal interests and needs.

In the first three chapters I set out the case for this curriculum and the establishment of four different types of colleges post-14, providing education and training in varying proportions.

In Chapter 4, Sir Mike Tomlinson, author of a famous report on 14–19 qualifications in England, makes a series of recommendations to establish a set of demanding vocational qualifications, reform GCSE and A-levels and create a Graduation Certificate, to be awarded to anyone who reaches a specified level in their academic, technical, vocational and apprenticeship studies, including the broader skills needed for success in further learning, work and adult life.

In Chapter 5, Professor Alan Smithers from the University of Buckingham, UK, describes the structures of education in other countries and makes the case for 14 to be the age of transfer in England, as it is in many other countries. He calls for an array of interconnected equivalent routes for 14–18-year-olds, leading to national qualifications in academic, technical and occupational subjects.

In Chapter 6, Professor Bob Schwartz from the Graduate School of Education at Harvard University, USA, outlines the main elements of a major report, *Pathways to Prosperity*, which he and colleagues wrote in response to the challenges facing American education. He argues for rigorous, robust pathways across the occupational spectrum that prepare young people for a life of satisfying work and further learning, and for an education system which gives young people the support and information needed to choose appropriate pathways. He strongly supports career academies and other programmes that meet the needs of students, especially those that engage students who might otherwise fall by the wayside.

In Chapter 7, Andrew Halls, Headmaster of Kings College School, Wimbledon, UK, explains the educational and developmental reasons why pupils in the English public school (fee-paying) system typically move between schools at 13+ and sets out the case for adapting our education system to respond to the different talents and abilities of our children and young people.

In Chapter 8, David Brandon-Bravo, headteacher of Parkfields Middle School in Bedfordshire, UK, draws on his direct experience of three-tier education to make a passionate case for the current and future role of middle schools in a reformed education system.

In Chapter 9, David Harbourne, Director of Research at the Edge Foundation, UK, and the Baker Dearing Educational Trust, UK, shows how other countries are improving their secondary level of education by recognizing that 14 is the key age of transfer. He highlights the success of Austria, which has one of the lowest levels of youth unemployment in Europe, and Ontario, which has for several years – and very successfully – treated 14–18 as a coherent phase of education.

In Appendix 1, David Harbourne describes the history of technical secondary education in our country since the mid-nineteenth century and how opportunities have repeatedly been lost to create a system which offers and values stretching combinations of academic and technical learning.

In Appendix 2, Nigel Wyatt, Executive Officer of the National Middle Schools' Forum, UK, sets out additional information about the history and strengths of English middle schools.

I would like to thank all the contributors to this book. Especial thanks and gratitude go to David Harbourne for all the excellent work he has done on this subject and for his editing of all the contributions, and to my secretary, Kathy Fogarty, for her patience in helping me prepare yet another book!

NOTES ON CONTRIBUTORS

Kenneth Baker is chairman of the Edge Foundation, UK, which champions technical, practical and vocational education, and of the Baker Dearing Educational Trust, UK, which is establishing a new network of University Technical Colleges in all regions of England. He was elected to Parliament in 1968 and was a junior minister in Edward Heath's government. He held a series of ministerial positions between 1981 and 1992, including three years as secretary of state for Education and Science (1986–9). He was home secretary from 1990 to 1992. In 1992, he became Lord Baker of Dorking and is an active member of the House of Lords.

David Brandon-Bravo is headteacher of Parkfields Middle School in Toddington, UK. Under his leadership, Parkfields has repeatedly been judged outstanding by the Office for Standards in Education, Children's Services and Skills (Ofsted). Other roles include president of the Bedfordshire Middle Schools and chief executive officer of the Harlington Area Schools Trust. He has worked for Central Bedfordshire local authority as a consultant headteacher and for the National College for School Leadership, UK, as a professional partner. David received a distinction in the Teaching Awards for Outstanding Headteacher of the Year, 2010.

Andrew Halls is headmaster of King's College School, Wimbledon, UK. He was previously head of English at Bristol Grammar School, deputy headmaster at Trinity School, and from 1998 until 2007 was master of Magdalen College School, Oxford. Magdalen College School was Sunday Times School of the Year in both 2004 and 2008. He won the Tatler award for Best Head of a Public School 2011–12.

David Harbourne is director of Policy and Research at the Edge Foundation, an independent education charity dedicated to raising the status of technical, practical and vocational learning. He is also senior education adviser to the Baker Dearing Educational Trust. After an early career in the civil service, he has worked in the field of vocational education and training in the United Kingdom for over 20 years, including senior positions with the National Association of Master Bakers, the Hospitality Training Foundation and the North Yorkshire Learning and Skills Council.

Robert B. Schwartz is Francis Keppel Professor of Practice of Educational Policy and Administration in the Graduate School of Education at Harvard University, USA. From 1997 to 2002, he was president of Achieve, Inc., an independent, non-profit organization created to help states improve their schools. From 1990 to 1996, he directed the education grant-making programme of the Pew Charitable Trusts, one of the USA's largest private philanthropies. He was previously a high-school English teacher and principal, and later executive director of the Boston Compact, a public–private partnership designed to improve access to higher education and employment for urban high-school graduates.

Alan Smithers is director of the Centre for Education and Employment Research at the University of Buckingham, UK. He has previously worked at a number of UK universities – as Sydney Jones Professor of Education at the University of Liverpool, Professor of Policy Research at Brunel University and Professor of Education at the University of Manchester. He has served on committees including the National Curriculum Council, the Beaumont Review of National Vocational Qualifications and the Royal Society Committee on Teacher Supply. Since 1997 he has been specialist adviser to the House of Commons Education Committee.

Mike Tomlinson is a leading British educationalist and chaired the Working Group on 14–19 Reform which reported to the Department for Education and Skills in 2004. He was Her Majesty's Chief Inspector for Schools from December 2000 until April 2002, during which time he was responsible for the work of Ofsted. From 2002 to 2007, he was chair of the Learning Trust, a not-for-profit body responsible for running the education services for Hackney, UK. He is a trustee of the Baker Dearing Educational Trust and was awarded a knighthood for services to education in 2005.

Nigel Wyatt has spent ten years supporting the development of middle
schools at a national level through his work as the executive officer of
the National Middle Schools' Forum. This followed a career as a maths
and technology teacher in middle schools in England. He combines his
role with work as an education consultant facilitating the development
of senior leaders in schools across the education service.

LIST OF ABBREVIATIONS

AS   Advanced Supplementary

AVCEs   Advanced Vocational Certificates of Education

BRIT   British Record Industry Trust

CBI   Confederation of British Industry

CEE   Certificate of Extended Education

CPVE   Certificate of Pre-Vocational Education

CSE   Certificate of Secondary Education

CTE   Career and Technical Education

EBac   English Baccalaureate

ECHS   Early College High Schools

FE   Further Education

GCSE   General Certificate of Secondary Education

GNVQ   General National Vocational Qualification

HE   Higher Education

HSTW   High Schools That Work

IB   International Baccalaureate

IBCC   International Baccalaureate Career-Related Certificate

ICT   Information and Communication Technology

IGCSE	International General Certificate of Secondary Education
JCQ	Joint Council for Qualifications
MBA	Master of Business Administration
MCS	Magdalen College School
NAF	National Academy Foundation
NEET	not in education, employment or training
NVQ	National Vocational Qualification
OCR	Oxford Cambridge and RSA Examinations
OECD	Organisation for Economic Co-operation and Development
Ofsted	Office for Standards in Education, Children's Services and Skills
ONS	Office for National Statistics
PGCE	Post Graduate Certificate in Education
PISA	Programme for International Student Assessment
ROSLA	Raising Of School Leaving Age
SHSM	Specialist High Skills Majors
TVEI	Technical and Vocational Education Initiative
UCAS	Universities and Colleges Admissions Service
UTC	University Technology College
VLE	Virtual Learning Environment
VRQ	Vocationally Related Qualifications
YA	Young Apprenticeship

1
TRANSFORMING 14–18 EDUCATION

Kenneth Baker

When I became Secretary of State for Education in 1986, I was convinced that the key to raising education standards across the country was a national curriculum.

Traditionally, headteachers decided the curriculum. However, children of broadly similar abilities were achieving widely different standards from one part of the country to the next and indeed from one school to the next. I was sure that a national curriculum would narrow the gap. In addition, I agreed wholeheartedly with my predecessor as Minister of Education Rab Butler who said that all children should go through a 'common mill' of education in order to acquire a shared – one might say, connective – knowledge of the country and world they live in.

However, if I had the task of fashioning the National Curriculum today, I would limit its scope to children aged 5 to 14.

Children need a clear grasp of the English language so that they can understand and be understood. They need a good understanding of arithmetic, which they will use at home, at work and even in sport and leisure. They need an appreciation of physics, chemistry and biology – subjects which are fundamental to our understanding of the world around us. They need to know about the country they live in: our history, culture and traditions. They need to be able to place Britain in context by studying world geography, world history and the cultures and religions of the world, and by learning languages other than English. In addition, children need to find out how things are made, how to use tools and resources, like the internet, how to express themselves through dance, theatre, music and art, and to discover their strengths, and indeed their weaknesses, on the playing field.

These are the foundations for life, work and further learning. They represent the knowledge, skills and experiences which, in my view, schools should provide for children up to the age of 14.

When we introduced the National Curriculum, however, young people were required to continue to study ten prescribed subjects up to the age of 16. I now see this as too ambitious, for three main reasons: it made the school timetable extremely crowded; it required young people to study subjects which some found uninteresting and uninspiring; and it severely limited opportunities for practical, hands-on learning.

Subsequent secretaries of state took steps to ease the pressure on the 14–16 curriculum. Indeed, the Labour government introduced the notion of a 14–19 'phase' of education and training. David Blunkett's green paper 'Schools: Building on Success' said:

> From 14, the curriculum will offer a significant degree of choice. Every pupil will still take GCSEs, but increasingly they will be able to mix academic and vocational GCSEs and work-based options. A variety of opportunities will be tailored to each person's aptitudes, abilities and preferences, but all will demand high standards. (Department for Education and Employment, 2001, p. 53)

This led to the appointment of the Working Group for 14–19 Reform, chaired by my friend and colleague Sir Mike Tomlinson. The Tomlinson Report, *14–19 Curriculum and Qualifications Reform*, published in 2004, was in my opinion one of the most important education reports received by the Labour government during its term of office. Its main recommendation was a fundamental reform of qualifications for 14–19-year-olds – in effect, the creation of a 14–19 curriculum. The report's main conclusions were rejected and in its place, we saw the development of a suite of occupationally related Diplomas, which have failed to find more than a toe-hold in a small number of schools and colleges. Since then, however, the law has been changed to require young people to remain in education or training until they are 17 from 2013, rising to 18 in 2015. This change has all-party support.

This must be the time to create a new vision for 14–18 education. Like Professor Alan Smithers, I prefer 14–18 to 14–19, as it more accurately captures the four years of compulsory education or training from age 14.

However, two things hold us back:

- the exaggerated importance of transition from primary to secondary education at the age of 11; and
- our fixation with exams at 16 – especially the GCSE.

The evolution of secondary education in England

In the closing years of the nineteenth century, a series of Acts of Parliament required children to attend school and provided state funding for elementary education up to the age of 13. However, there was no statutory entitlement to state-funded education beyond this age and very few parents had the means to pay for their children to attend fee-paying grammar and public schools.

The Education Act 1902 established local education authorities and gave them the right to establish, maintain and fund secondary schools. This led inevitably to questions about what should be taught in these new secondary schools. The 1904 Secondary Regulations provided the answer: a general education comprising English language and literature, geography, history, a foreign language, mathematics, science, drawing, handicraft and physical training. The secondary curriculum was, in short, based very largely on the grammar and public school curriculum developed by Thomas Arnold and his followers during the nineteenth century.

The school leaving age was raised to 14 after the First World War, based on a belief that children needed more and better education to equip them for life in the modern world. In most cases, this meant staying on at an elementary school rather than transferring to a secondary school – which was the case for my own father who won a book prize at the age of 14 from his elementary school in Newport.

Some thought this unsatisfactory, and argued for a clearer definition of education for older children. Sir William Hadow was appointed to chair a consultative committee on 'The Education of the Adolescent', which reached this conclusion in 1926:

> There is a tide which begins to rise in the veins of youth at the age of eleven or twelve. It is called by the name of adolescence.
>
> . . . We desire to abolish the word 'elementary', and to alter and extend the sense of the word 'secondary'. . . . We propose to substitute the term 'primary', but to restrict the use of that term to the period of education which ends at the age of eleven or twelve. To the period of education which follows upon it we would give the name secondary. (Board of Education, 1927, p. xxi)

Relatively little progress had been made by the start of the Second World War, and the issue was revisited by the Educational Reconstruction Committee of the Board of Education in 1940–1.

There was general agreement that the school leaving age should be raised again, initially to 15, and that England should implement a tripartite system of post-primary education consisting of selective grammar schools, selective technical schools and modern schools.

There was, however, less agreement about the age at which children should transfer to these schools. The technical branch of the Board of Education favoured transfer at 13, but the secondary branch held out for selection at 11+, so as to keep intact what had become the standard five-year grammar school course for 11–16-year-olds.

The matter was settled by the permanent secretary in March 1941 'on the basis that the implementation of transfer at 13+ would take many years to achieve, whereas transfer at 11+ could be secured within five' (Richardson and Wiborg, 2010, p. 6).

In short, this decision – which has had huge and lasting repercussions – was taken for essentially pragmatic reasons. In effect, the starting age for grammar schools settled the matter.

Age of transfer settled, the next question was how to allocate children to different types of secondary school. Educational psychologists claimed it was possible to use a battery of tests to establish the academic potential of all 11-year-olds. The 11+, as it came to be known, formed the basis for allocating children to grammar, technical and secondary modern schools after the 1944 Education Act.

Selective technical schools never really got off the ground. There were 317 in 1946 and while a few new ones were established in the years that followed, others closed or merged with neighbouring schools. In 1955, R. A. Butler commented upon the number of technical schools: 'There are too few of these schools and too many of them are poked away in corners of technical colleges, and are failing to receive proper recognition and support' (quoted in Edwards, 1960, p. 5). How right he was; but he was unable to arrest their decline. Quite frankly they were killed by snobbery – parents wanted their children to go to the school on the hill – the grammar – and not the one in town which they associated with greasy rags and dirty jobs.

At the same time, confidence in the 11+ started to diminish during the 1950s. A significant number of children in secondary modern schools turned out to be capable of passing O-levels, while a significant number of children in grammar schools turned out to be capable of failing them. This growing unease paved the way for the introduction of comprehensive education in most parts of England.

The policy of comprehensive secondary education started with Antony Crosland's famous circular of 1965 which urged local education authorities to replace the tripartite system with a national system of comprehensive schools. Looking back, it seems extraordinary that such a fundamental change could be introduced without formal consultation or primary legislation, but so it was.

In the following years, over 1,000 grammar schools were abolished under Labour and Conservative governments. The education minister who signed the greatest number of death warrants was Margaret Thatcher – an episode in her career of which she did not like to be reminded.

The comprehensive movement, which had its roots in the thinking of socialists, like Professor Tawney in the 1920s, was based on the belief that the advantages of birth, wealth, privilege and social position available to some children could only be eliminated if all children, irrespective of ability and background, went to the same school in the same neighbourhood at the same time. This policy of common access was driven as much by social engineering as by any educational considerations.

Interestingly, the push for comprehensive education provided a brief moment when 11 ceased to be the only age of transfer in some parts of the country. Many local authorities had a significant number of small secondary schools. Expanding some while abandoning others would have been more expensive than adopting a new three-tier system of education, comprising first schools, middle schools and high schools.

Middle schools typically catered for children aged 8–12 or 9–13. Legislation to permit transfer at ages other than 11 was passed in 1964, and the concept of the middle school gained further support in the 1967 Plowden Report, *Children and Their Primary Schools* (Department of Education and Science). At their peak, there were 1,800 middle schools in England and Wales, as shown in Figure 1.1.

Within a few years, however, local authorities started to abandon the three-tier system. The main reason was surplus capacity, caused by falling numbers of children of school age. The Audit Commission estimated that in 1990, there were 900,000 surplus places in English and Welsh primary schools, including many in middle schools straddling the primary/secondary divide (p. 5). It was said that eliminating these places would save £140 million a year. As a consequence, most local authorities followed the path of restoring two-tier education system. By 2011, 215 middle schools remained, spread across 19 local authority areas. It is safe to say that transfer at 11 again rules supreme.

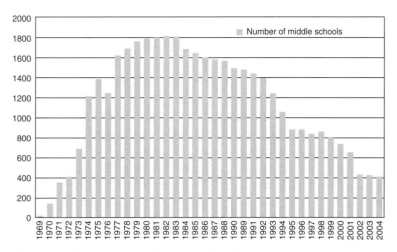

Figure 1.1 Middle schools in England, 1969–2004.
Source: National Middle Schools Forum

Source data:

Year	Number of middle schools	Year	Number of middle schools
1969	15	1987	1584
1970	140	1988	1567
1971	349	1989	1493
1972	409	1990	1481
1973	687	1991	1438
1974	1213	1992	1395
1975	1382	1993	1241
1976	1245	1994	1058
1977	1627	1995	883
1978	1690	1996	885
1979	1764	1997	840
1980	1789	1998	860
1981	1800	1999	806
1982	1816	2000	734
1983	1810	2001	654
1984	1687	2002	432
1985	1645	2003	425
1986	1604	2004	409

The influence of exams at 16

The very existence of three-tier education in some parts of England – and in other countries, too, such as Germany and the United States – shows that there is nothing sacrosanct about transfer from primary to secondary education at the age of 11. As we have seen, however, many local authorities abandoned three-tier structures both to save money at a time of falling school rolls, and to align their structures with the system of Key Stages which I introduced over 25 years ago.

Looking back at what has happened since then, it is clear that Key Stage 3 (age 11–14) and Key Stage 4 (age 14–16) are now bracketed together in the minds of most children, teachers, parents and politicians: their shared purpose is to prepare children for GCSEs at 16.

This has skewed public, political and media perceptions of the aims of education. We have lost sight of the need to find and support the talents and ambitions of each young person and instead, we focus relentlessly on a single measure: the achievement of five GCSEs at grades A* to C, including English and maths.

It is little wonder that schools start to track pupils' progress towards GCSEs from as early as Year 7; and while external tests (SATs) are no longer set for 14-year-olds, teachers have continued to assess each pupil's progress in the following subjects at the end of Key Stage 3 (age 14):

- English
- Maths
- Science
- History
- Geography
- Modern foreign languages
- Design and technology
- Information and Communication Technology (ICT)
- Art and design
- Music
- Physical education
- Citizenship
- Religious education.

In 2004, David Blunkett introduced greater flexibility into the Key Stage 4 curriculum in order to accommodate the aptitudes, abilities and preferences of each student.

It is widely assumed that this flexibility resulted in a mass exodus from the traditional curriculum. In reality, subjects taught as part of the Key Stage 3 National Curriculum continue to dominate choices at Key Stage 4. In June 2011, the subjects listed above accounted for 88 per cent of all GCSE entries. The take-up of other subjects was much more limited than one might imagine. Indeed in some subjects, take-up is worryingly low: for example, there were only 1,850 entries for GCSE engineering in June 2011 (data from JCQ, 2011).

Of course, GCSEs are not the only qualifications taken at the end of Key Stage 4. According to statistics quoted in the Wolf Report on Vocational Education, over 587,000 vocationally related qualifications (VRQs) such as BTECs and OCR Nationals were taken at the end of Key Stage 4 in 2009–10 (Wolf, 2011, p. 57).

Nevertheless, GCSEs in National Curriculum subjects continue to dominate the landscape to a greater degree than widely realized, as shown in Figure 1.2.

The Labour government introduced greater flexibility into the Key Stage 4 curriculum in 2004. It also invested heavily in Diplomas in the hope of creating a high-quality alternative to GCSEs.

In reality, other VRQs, including BTECs, OCR Nationals and ASDAN certificates, proved more popular. In 2004, just under 13,000 VRQs were awarded. As we have seen, this figure had grown to 587,000 by 2010.

This rapid increase was achieved at considerable cost to the reputation of vocational education. Some schools steered young people towards VRQs to boost their position in the league tables, not because they were necessarily the best option for individual students. In addition, the quality of teaching was sometimes poor, with technical subjects being taught by non-specialists and without access to appropriate facilities and equipment. Ofsted also called into question some assessment methods.

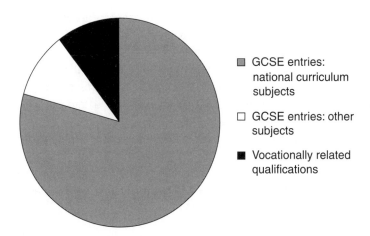

Figure 1.2 GCSE and vocationally related qualification entries at the end of Key Stage 4, 2009–10.
Source: JCQ 2010 and Wolf 2011

Source data
GCSE entries: national curriculum subjects 4,557,705
GCSE entries: other subjects 594,265
Vocationally related qualifications 587,000

In response to the Wolf Review of Vocational Education, Michael Gove, Secretary of State for Education in the coalition government, set in train a series of reforms designed to rebuild confidence in a reduced range of vocational qualifications for 14–16-year-olds. He also introduced the English Baccalaureate (EBac), which recognizes the achievement of GCSE grades A* to C in traditional academic subjects: English, maths, science, foreign languages (ancient and modern), history and geography. As a consequence from 2012 there will be a decline in the number of technical GCSEs, and a marked decline in vocationally related qualifications such as BTECs and OCR Nationals. Vocational education risks being largely squeezed out of pre-16 education.

Within months, however, the spotlight was also turned on the quality of GCSEs. Awarding organizations (formerly known as exam boards) came under scrutiny following claims about weak content, lax standards, grade inflation and collusion between examiners and teachers. All this was said to stem – at least in part – from the pre-eminence of GCSE success rates in school league tables, because schools were under pressure to improve results year-on-year. A-levels have come under similar attack. Universities claim that rising numbers of top grades make it increasingly difficult to distinguish between applicants, while universities and employers alike bemoan poor standards of literacy and numeracy even among students with good grades.

I entirely agree that quality and rigour should be at the heart of all teaching and every qualification. It is right that reforms should tackle malpractice and restore public confidence in the integrity of our qualifications system.

At the same time, there is a risk that we lose sight of issues which are just as important. I am especially concerned that we will – yet again – turn our backs on practical, technical and vocational education. It is a mistake we have been making for well over a century; it is a mistake we must not make again.

The importance of learning by doing

In the past, left-handedness was regarded as unnatural – something to be repressed. Many young people were actually punished for writing with their left hands.

Left-handedness is now accepted as entirely natural. But we still regard an interest in and aptitude for working with the hands as something to be discouraged, particularly among young people adept at verbal reasoning and so-called academic learning. I would argue that this is a form of discrimination almost on a par with old-fashioned attitudes to left-handedness.

When students are given the opportunity to learn through their hands as well as their brains, the immediate and practical become part of their lives and their passion for learning is engaged. Through working with materials like metal, wood and plastics, and by working on projects and in teams, students quickly appreciate how vital it is to master mathematical and linguistic skills.

Self-esteem arises by acquiring not just knowledge but also acquiring a competence. Many young people often win that competence, along with the self-esteem and peer recognition which earns them respect, through excelling at sport. Some can do it through exceptional scholarship but many others could do this if they had the opportunity to acquire a useful skill that led to material things which could be made, repaired and maintained. Yet in schools today, many of the manual skills that are necessary to achieve this are simply not available or else provided in a watered-down and minor way.

In the grammar school I attended in Lancashire in the late 1940s we had two hours of carpentry a week. I still retain vivid memories of those practical lessons: indeed I cannot remember anything else I learnt there, though it was a very good school. This sort of learning experience has largely disappeared from grammar schools and many of today's academies – especially those which converted to academy status after the election of the coalition government in 2010.

This suppression is partly due to the belief held for several decades that a computerized, knowledge-based economy will provide a massive number of jobs for knowledge workers. But this has proven to be a misguided optimism as we have discovered that many of these jobs can be done just as easily and more cheaply abroad.

There is a second reason why practical skills training has been downgraded. Comprehensive egalitarian theories of education are based in part on the fear that enabling youngsters to acquire a specific skill at school limits their future opportunities and dooms them to a lesser position in our society. In contrast the feeling has spread that going to university is the only pathway to success. Any engineering company will tell you, however, that most of the graduate engineers they seek to employ lack practical skills and do not have the capacity to use basic tools.

In his book *The Case for Working with Your Hands*, Professor Matthew Crawford says the skilled trades involve 'cognitive richness', adding: 'Skilled manual labour entails a systematic encounter with the material world, precisely the kind of encounter that gives rise to natural science' (2009, p. 21).

There needs to be no divide between thinking and doing, between mental and manual. The motor mechanic and the surgeon are valued because they have manual skills as well as the mental capacity, education and understanding to diagnose the problems that their customers and patients present to them.

Furthermore, mastering a skill does not deny the successful student the opportunity to go to university and engage in higher education (HE). Skills and knowledge are not mutually exclusive: on the contrary, they are mutually complementary. When students apply knowledge to a specific problem, they are more likely to understand and remember key concepts.

Lessons from research

First, it is intriguing to learn that intelligence – as measured by IQ – can change over time. Writing in 'Nature', a team from the Wellcome Trust Centre for Neuroimaging reported evidence that both verbal and non-verbal IQ can rise or fall in the teenage years. Further, this is closely correlated with changes in local brain structure: verbal IQ can be linked to the motor speech region of the brain, and performance (non-verbal) IQ to the motor hand region close to the anterior cerebellum region. The research sample was small – 33 individuals – but the authors suggest their findings may have significant implications for education: 'The implication of our present findings is that an individual's strengths and weaknesses in skills relevant to education and employment are still emerging or changing in the teenage years' (Ramsden et al., 2011, p. 115).

This implies that we should be particularly careful to structure education so as to develop both the motor *speech* region and the motor *hand* region. By delivering a largely academic curriculum to most children and young people, we may actually inhibit the development of the motor hand region, harming the prospects of young people whose natural talents are technical and practical.

Young people should therefore be exposed to a range of topics, subjects, experiences and styles of learning, which will help them decide who they are, who they want to be, what they like doing and where their strengths lie. We need people whose strengths include working with their hands and solving practical problems as much as we need people who can use facts and language.

Second, we should also remember that IQ measures a particular type of intelligence – mainly based on the use of language and the analysis of patterns. Other forms of intelligence tend not to be assessed by the education system, nor greatly appreciated by our policy makers.

Robert Sternberg has developed a theory of 'successful intelligence', which combines analytical, creative and practical intelligence. After many years of applying his theory to practical situations, Sternberg concluded:

> The educational system in the United States, as in many countries, places great emphasis on instruction and assessments that tap into two important skills: memory and analysis. Students who are adept in these two skills tend to profit from the educational system because the ability tests, instruction, and achievement tests we use all largely measure products and processes emanating from these two kinds of skills. There is a problem, however – namely, that children whose strengths are in other kinds of skills may be shortchanged by this system. (2011, p. 523)

Third, we need to challenge the assumption that academically talented young people should study only academic subjects, in purely academic ways.

Richardson and Sing (2011) conducted fieldwork in six secondary schools in England and Wales. They explored the impact of practical learning on young people aged 11–16 who had already shown themselves to be academically able – that is, young people who were destined to do well in their GCSE exams and, most likely, in A-levels too.

Their research provided clear evidence that practical and applied learning has a strong and positive effect on the motivation and achievement of academically able students. Many young people are able to do equally well in English and engineering, in history and design.

This is not exactly surprising. Give talented and motivated young people an interesting challenge and they will rise to it. Ask them to combine mental agility with a practical task, and they can do it. If this were not the case, we would have no talented surgeons, inventors or engineers.

However, Williamson and Sing also found that a great majority of academically able students gravitate to more abstract and analytical learning as they progress through the teenage years. The main reason is cultural. These young people are destined for university, and achievement in traditional subjects is widely used when selecting candidates for high-status university places.

In summary, we have created a system and a society which favours one form of learning over another. I believe the time has come to change this perception, once and for all. People have talents, abilities and preferences. We must support them all, starting at school.

2

A NEW VISION FOR EDUCATION IN ENGLAND

Kenneth Baker

In Chapter 1, I said that if I had the task of fashioning the National Curriculum today, I would limit its scope to children up to the age of 14: what we currently know as Key Stages 1 to 3. The current configuration of Key Stages is illustrated in Table 2.1.

In 2011, the Secretary of State for Education Michael Gove invited an expert panel to review the National Curriculum. The panel recommended that Key Stage 2 should be further divided into lower Key Stage 2 (age 7–9) and upper Key Stage 2 (9–11). They said:

> the four year span of Key Stage 2, as currently configured, is too long and . . . can result in a lack of pace and ambition in Years 4 and 5 (ages 8–10). We recommend that that present Key Stage 2 be split in two to form two new Key Stages each of two years duration. (Department for Education, 2011b, p. 8)

They went on to argue that this change

> would also facilitate age-appropriate innovation in forms of school organisation, including the possible use of more subject specialists in Upper Key Stage 2. In the consultations with key primary organisations, primary education practitioners and others to date, the proposal has been supported. (Department for Education, 2011b, p. 31)

Table 2.1 Current school year/Key Stage structure

School year (age)	Key Stage
1 (5/6)	1
2 (6/7)	
3 (7/8)	2
4 (8/9)	
5 (9/10)	
6 (10/11)	
7 (11/12)	3
8 (12/13)	
9 (13/14)	
10 (14/15)	4
11 (15/16)	

The panel was less sure about the duration of Key Stages 3 and 4: instead, they set out the pros and cons of a 2:3 year split against the current norm, 3:2. However, they did not propose the further integration of post-16 education into the overall structure, despite plans to require all 17- and 18-year-olds to stay in education or training after 2015.

If the panel's proposals for Key Stage 2 were implemented, we would in effect move from four Key Stages to five – or, if 16–18 education and training is included, six. In the new scheme, five Key Stages would last two years and one, three years. While I agree that the age of 9 should be viewed as a watershed, I believe we should simplify, not complicate, the structure of compulsory education.

An alternative vision

I propose that we provide education in three phases: 5–9 (primary), 9–14 (middle) and 14–18 (secondary). It will be necessary to establish a phase extending to 18 when, in 2015, it becomes a statutory requirement for all young people to remain in education or training until they are 18.

In my vision of the future, the National Curriculum would set out the aims, objectives and broad content of education for two of the three phases, primary and middle.

Primary education must focus on the essentials, including in particular reading, writing, speech and basic arithmetic. It is also a period when essential social skills are developed and embedded. Much teaching in the primary phase 5–9 is in a single class with one teacher. This is important both for children's education and for their social development.

However, most children go through puberty between the ages of 9 and 14. It is a period of rapid development and for many, acute self-consciousness. They see themselves, quite naturally, as different from younger children. At the same time, they may benefit from being kept at arm's length from the sometimes dubious influence of older teenagers. This is an important argument for seeing 9–14 as a separate phase of education.

There is already a model for this: the middle school. The history and benefits of middle schools are discussed fully by David Brandon-Bravo in Chapter 8 and by Nigel Wyatt in Appendix 2.

Middle schools enjoyed a period of rapid expansion from 1969 to 1983, followed by a decline. However, they have not disappeared entirely. Their supporters claim several distinct advantages, including separation from younger children and older teenagers. It is claimed, too, that levels of commitment and attainment are easier to manage in a middle school than in an 11–16 or 11–18 secondary school.

In addition, middle schools allow an earlier introduction to specialist teaching and subject disciplines. In the 1960s, the Plowden Report recommended that middle schools should have teachers skilled in certain areas of the curriculum rather than in single subjects. In 1992 the 'three wise men', Robin Alexander, Jim Rose and Chris Woodhead, called for a stronger emphasis on subject teaching in Years 5 and 6 (ages 9–11), saying: 'Every primary school should, in principle, have direct access to specialist expertise in all nine National Curriculum subjects and in religious education' (Alexander et al., 1992, p. 2). As noted already, the expert panel on the National Curriculum also supports increased specialization from age 9.

Middle schools already provide for the gradual introduction of subject specialists. In addition, they have specialist facilities and equipment such as science labs.

In future, the primary and middle phases of education could be provided in two ways: primary schools for children aged 5–9 and entirely separate 9–14 middle schools; or all-through schools from 5–14, accommodating both age groups on a shared site but with dual identities – primary and middle. In either case, the period from 9 to 14 should be more subject-based, and the single teacher should gradually be replaced by a team.

In their time at middle school, young people should study core National Curriculum subjects, discover their strengths and gradually form an idea of the direction they want to take at 14. They should find out about future options through visits to further and higher education institutions and discussions with current students, apprentices and people from across the world of work. They and their parents should have access to information, advice and guidance about the vast range of career and learning choices that lie ahead.

There would be a clear end point at 14 when young people select, with the advice of their teachers and the help of their parents, the secondary education best suited to their interests and talents.

Secondary education

In the early years of the twenty-first century, the Labour government introduced the concept of a 14–19 phase of education. The Tomlinson Report of 2004, which was one of the most important received by that government, proposed a framework of qualifications which would provide continuity, choice and coherence to this new 'phase'.

Subsequent reforms have, however, only gone part of the way to making Tomlinson's vision a reality. As we saw in Chapter 1, the vast majority of young people study a large number of mainly academic subjects during Key Stage 4 (ages 14–16), and take exams in most of them. Indeed, some take the same exams several times because of the pressure for schools to tick the box marked 'grade C or above' before they reach the age of 16. There is little time to enrich learning through visits, experiments, projects and off-timetable activities. Further, the system forces young people to focus on listening, reading and writing at the expense of more practical, hands-on learning.

Once they are 16, however, young people drop most subjects entirely. Those who take A-levels typically study no more than four subjects at 16, and many drop one of these a year later. Those who choose technical and vocational subjects may study only one or two subjects. It is hardly surprising that post-16 programmes are widely criticized as lacking breadth.

The solution is surely clear: a single phase of 14–18 education in which young people study a variety of subjects to a greater or lesser degree of depth, over a time span of four years, and adapted to their individual talents and preferred styles of learning.

This makes all the more sense because young people will be legally required to stay in education or training until they are 18 from 2015 onwards. This change enjoys cross-party support. Just as importantly, it has the support of the teaching profession, most employers and the majority of young people themselves. It would reflect not only the private sector pattern but also the clear needs of many students who, at the age of 13–14, are looking to a range of studies that will lead them to the world of work. There could be no better time to establish a new vision for upper secondary education and create the structures to support it.

14 is not too soon to make a wise decision

Elsewhere in the world, young people are trusted to make wise choices at 14. Here, we seem to think choices should be delayed at least to the age of 16.

However, there is evidence that we have underestimated young people's ability to make decisions. Commenting on research which involved listening to 245 boys aged 11–14 from 12 secondary schools in London, Frosh et al. wrote:

> The image of the angrily grunting and inarticulate teenager is not one which stands up to scrutiny when one looks at what can happen when boys are given the opportunity to reflect on their experiences

and are encouraged to talk. It is worthy of note that almost all the boys who were interviewed individually became engaged in very thoughtful and rich discussions with the interviewer. (2003, p. 87)

I was not in the least surprised by this finding. Historically, our education system required young teenagers to make important decisions at an early age. Up until 1918 most had to leave school at 12, for it was only in that year the school leaving age was raised to 14. My own grandfather left school at 12 and had to make his own way in the world for he was at the early end of his formal education, but that did not prevent him becoming a manager in Newport Docks during the Second World War.

I am convinced that most young people are ready to choose between styles and types of learning by the time they are 14. University Technical Colleges (which I describe in more detail in Chapter 3) have shown they can recruit highly motivated young people at 14 who know that they enjoy practical and technical learning. Early results, not least from the JCB Academy in Staffordshire, show that they go on to do exceptionally well – better, in fact, than previously predicted. At the same time, it is important that choices do not lead to dead ends and that it is possible for a student to change routes at 16. This is achieved by all students studying a broad curriculum alongside and illustrated by the specialist education they have chosen.

Provided we arm them with the right, objective information, therefore, we should trust young people to make wise choices.

14–18 secondary education: four pathways

Existing 11–16 and 11–18 comprehensives and academies will not find it easy to provide a full range of educational experience from traditional academic study to effective technical education, to the performing and creative arts, or to vocational career based subjects. Students may be given a taste of each but their appetite for in-depth, focused learning linked to their particular interests simply could not be accommodated because of the restrictions of space, specialist teaching and equipment needed.

Instead, I believe we should be moving towards four distinct 14–18 pathways:

- a technical pathway, providing expert teaching and hands-on learning in subjects such as engineering and ICT;

- a liberal arts pathway built around, but not wholly limited to, general subjects – what we often call 'academic' subjects;

- a sports and creative arts pathway, embracing a wide range of sports and arts ranging from theatre, music and dance to fine art and a wide range of hand crafts such as pottery, sculpture and cabinet-making;

- a career pathway, similar to the dual system found in Austria, Germany and more recently (and to a limited extent) in Ontario. It would also be similar to the career and technical schools found in many American cities such as New York. This pathway would combine basic academic subjects with work-based apprenticeship and off-the-job education and training.

These pathways are described in more detail in Chapter 3.

Picture 2.1 Engineering at the JCB Academy, Rocester.

University Technical Colleges provide a pattern for what I have in mind. By the end of 2012, 5 will have opened, and a further 28 have been given approval to open in 2013 and 2014 right across England. There is certainly sufficient demand for a 100 to be established. With each UTC enrolling 600 students across four year groups, this means over 60,000 students would then be studying at UTCs. UTCs are not just interesting experiments: they have become a movement.

The common entitlement

Learning from experience in many other countries, I support the introduction of a broad common entitlement for all 14–18-year-olds in England. All young people should achieve sound English and maths skills. All should appreciate their place in society and the world. All should be curious about the way things are made, who invented them and how science and technology shapes our lives.

A broad entitlement is quite different from a detailed National Curriculum. The 'what, how and when' of secondary education must be fluid. It must accommodate and support the talents, ambitions and preferred styles of learning of our young people. It must support the aims we need in a modern world:

- breadth of knowledge and understanding;
- strong English and maths, including oral communication and mental arithmetic;
- less emphasis on high-stakes testing and league tables at 16 in favour of cumulative performance over a four-year period;
- practical, technical and vocational options available to young people of all abilities: they should not be seen simplistically as a last resort for the least able;
- young people who prefer practical, technical and vocational styles of learning should also have opportunities to achieve success in more academic disciplines, linked to their chosen specialist field;
- opportunities to progress to further and higher education, apprenticeships and work.

As Professor Wolf has argued, English and maths are fundamental to young people's employment and education prospects (2011, p. 8). A significant advantage of my new vision for secondary education is that English and maths – and other subjects, too – can be taught in ways which link them firmly to the student's chosen pathway. Concepts are more readily mastered when put into context, such as calculating the number of bricks needed to build a wall, the amount of pressure to move a piston up and down, the weight of a bridge or the speed of a moving object. Where this already happens, teachers report improvements in students' understanding and progress in both maths and English.

However, it is very difficult to deliver tailored learning in the present circumstances. This was one of the lessons learned from the ill-fated experiment with Diplomas. Each Diploma comprised principal learning linked to a broad occupational sector, supported by compulsory English, maths and ICT, work experience, a project and optional elements. In principle, it should have been possible to adapt the maths and English curriculum so that each was taught in the context of the chosen Diploma: maths for engineering or hospitality, English for business administration or construction and so on.

In practice, it was virtually impossible to do this when there were only small groups of students following each Diploma. Students received their practical training in a separate building usually provided by the local further education (FE) college and returned to their school for English and maths. Studies were not meshed together, and it was utterly impractical to tailor each lesson to the interests of three, four or five different Diplomas in a single lesson.

However, the problem becomes less acute when larger numbers choose a particular pathway. We are already seeing this in UTCs: UTCs teach German for engineering, not Goethe; the history of industry and technology; the geography of world trade. I see this as a model for the future, in which all young people continue to be offered a broad common entitlement embracing English, maths, science, foreign languages and humanities alongside – and tailored to – their specialist options.

Furthermore, treating 14–18 as a single phase allows us to break down the artificial barrier currently in place at age 16. Maths and English can be taught beyond the age of 16, giving late developers more time to achieve good results while those who are achieving well can accelerate their progress in the context of their chosen route.

We must not neglect the wider social skills which prepare young people for adult life. These are sometimes given a particular name, such as 'employability skills' or 'personal learning and thinking skills'. In practice, they are skills, qualities and attributes which people use at home, at work and in the community, such as empathy – understanding other people's points of view – and communication – not just talking, but listening too. Similarly, everyone needs to be able to reflect on what they have learned not only in the classroom but also from personal experience. Teamwork and problem-solving come under the same heading, together with instruction in financial, business and enterprise skills. The new secondary entitlement should support the development of these skills and attributes in every child, in every school.

Implications for the school estate

Transforming the school estate to accommodate three-tier education will not be easy. However, it has been done before. About 1,500 middle schools were opened in the 1960s and 1970s, but following the 1990 Audit Commission report on surplus school places, many were closed. Nevertheless, many middle schools remain open in 2012, in 19 different local authority areas. We have not lost the template.

Furthermore, we are starting to see a surge in the number of children starting school in England. The birth rate rose by 20 per cent between 2002 and 2010, and this is already reflected in growing demand for places in primary schools in England. Numbers in state-maintained nursery and state-funded primary schools started increasing in 2010 and are expected to continue rising: by the end of the decade, pupil numbers are projected to reach levels last seen in the late 1970s (Department for Education, 2011a). At the risk of stating the obvious, these pupils will in due course move up through our education system, putting pressure not only on primary schools but on secondary schools as well. Secondary schools will start to feel the effects of rising pupil numbers from 2016 onwards. This may provide the ideal opportunity to restore three-tier education.

In a large city with good public transport connections, it would be possible to reconfigure the school estates in much the same way as when middle schools were introduced. In some cases, school buildings might be divided, so that primary and middle schools could share a single campus for 5–14-year-olds. What was once an 11–16 comprehensive might now become a middle school. A larger 11–18 school might become a sports and performing arts college, a career college, a liberal arts college or a university technical college.

In smaller towns and more rural areas, there would be a need for greater flexibility. In the 1950s, there were bilateral and trilateral schools, with grammar, technical and modern education offered under one roof. Some specialist facilities, such as science labs, were shared. A similar approach could be taken today, so that middle schools could share facilities with secondary colleges offering more than one pathway.

I am under no illusion that this represents a major upheaval. A start could be made by establishing a cluster of secondary schools in our towns and cities, some starting at 11, others like UTCs and Studio Schools starting at 14: indeed, this is the pattern that is beginning to emerge in Liverpool. It would be in the interest of the 11–18 schools to recognize that some of their students would be able to make much more progress if they were able to attend a college for students aged 14–18. However, we have consistently shied away from doing the right thing in this country. If we want an education system fit for the twenty-first century, we must be prepared to make it happen.

3

THE 14–18 PATHWAYS

Kenneth Baker

The technical pathway: the University Technical College

My ideas for the technical pathway are greatly influenced by work which I started with my friend, the late Ron Dearing, a few years ago. Dearing was not only a great public servant, he also had a deep understanding of the power of education and its capacity to bring out the potential of all our young people.

Dearing attended a technical school. Compared with grammar schools – and even compared with secondary modern schools – technical schools were the least developed arm of the tripartite education system introduced following the 1944 Education Act. But Dearing and I always regretted their passing. Between us, therefore, we came up with ideas for a latter day and better equivalent: the University Technical College, or UTC.

I see the UTC curriculum as providing a model not just for the technical pathway but for others too. The key to each pathway is motivation: every young person must have access to programmes which will engage their talents, stretch and enthuse them and prepare them for further learning and work. Each pathway must be supported by specialist teachers, equipment and facilities. Each must offer a broad range of courses and programmes, with students opting to focus on a chosen specialist field for some of their time. As I outline in Chapter 2, they will study core subjects including English and maths in the context of their chosen

Picture 3.1 JCB Academy, Rocester.

specialism. And through a credit-based approach, they will accumulate solid evidence of success in each year from age 14 onwards.

UTCs are therefore forerunners for the secondary education I believe we need in this country. They are 14–18 schools which offer technical subjects taught to a high level by experienced professionals using state-of-the-art equipment and facilities. They are different from the technical schools of the 1940s and 1950s in three ways:

1. A UTC recruits at 14, as we believe that young people at that age can decide, with the help of their teachers and parents, where their interests lie. However, the education and training they receive must not be exclusively, or even predominantly, technical, so that if they discover that this type of education is not suitable for them they can transfer to another school.

2. Each UTC is sponsored by a university which helps to shape the curriculum and assist in pupil teaching and mentoring. The path therefore lies open for students to go on to foundation and higher degrees. Universities also enhance the status of these colleges in the eyes of their students, their parents, the business world and society in general.

3. Local employers are also sponsors, helping to shape the curriculum and giving the students a real-life experience of

companies operating in the technical and engineering world. Some provide apprenticeships post-16, some create projects which teams work on and some provide teaching modules.

UTCs enjoy cross-party support. Lord Adonis was the first minister to recognize their potential and he authorized the development of the first two to open their doors. The coalition government took up the baton in 2010 and pledged support for at least 24 UTCs across the country by 2015. They have proved to be so popular that by June 2012, 33 had been approved and there is a pent-up demand for at least a further 60. I have never known so much enthusiasm from so many people, in so many parts of the country and from all political persuasions.

Some commentators have forecast that UTCs will offer their students a narrow curriculum. That is not the case. Between 14 and 16, students spend 40 per cent of their time on technical studies and 60 per cent on other, general subjects including English, maths and science. They also learn a foreign language, but the course content will be tailored to the technical subject being studied: German for engineering, not Goethe; French for business, not Molière. They also study humanities: the history of engineering, inventions and great scientific breakthroughs or the geography of industrial and commercial expansion.

After 16, the percentages are reversed. Students continue to study outside the core technical curriculum, having the opportunity to study for A-levels and to develop wider employability, enterprise, financial and business skills. This ensures they are able to keep future options open. On leaving a UTC, students may choose apprenticeships, FE or university, depending on their ambitions and interests.

The breadth and richness of the curriculum is only possible as UTCs have extended the daily attendance time from 08.30 to 17.00 and are open for 40 weeks instead of 38. This increased time adds a whole additional teaching year over the time students spend there.

The first UTC, supported by JCB, opened in September 2010 in Rocester, Staffordshire. There has been remarkable success even in these early days:

First, behaviour has improved. In large part this is because students are treated as adults, wear business dress and each has their own laptop or iPad. Just as importantly, they learn subjects they are interested in. Truancy and disruptive behaviour have decreased considerably. The disinterested and disengaged become interested and involved.

Second, as English and maths are blended into specialist training there has been significant improvement in these two subjects.

Third, UTCs are agents of social mobility. The students come from all backgrounds and all abilities. They give to many the second chance opportunity that the grammar school provided 40 or 50 years ago.

Fourth, the employability of students is significantly enhanced. The JCB Academy has completed two years and about a third of the students at 16 plan to leave, all of whom have the promise of jobs, apprenticeships or courses at other institutions.

Fifth, several of JCB's post-16 students have been offered university places. Interestingly, two students have turned down offers from Russell Group universities in order to take up higher apprenticeships, which lead to foundation degrees.

Case study: the Black Country UTC

Picture 3.2 The Black Country University Technical College, Walsall.

The Black Country UTC opened in 2011 to give 14–18-year-olds with an interest in science and engineering the chance to learn and succeed in an inspirational institution, using the latest technology that industry has to offer and supported by expert staff.

From the outset, the UTC benefited from partnerships with the University of Wolverhampton, Walsall College, the Institution of Mechanical Engineers and employers including Siemens, National Grid and Chamberlin and Hill (a world-class engineering and castings business).

The aim of the Black Country curriculum is to give students insights into the very wide range of careers open to people with high-level knowledge and skills in science and engineering. Students are not trained to do a specific job, but to prepare for the next step – whether that is an apprenticeship, full-time FE or a degree.

Teaching is built round exciting and challenging real-world projects and developing innovative new products and processes that could change the way we live in the future. Students gain knowledge and skills which will fit them for the future, including problem-solving, group working on projects, presentation skills and an enterprising attitude.

The curriculum is actively shaped by employers. Siemens were especially closely engaged in designing the engineering curriculum and were so keen to see this implemented that they donated equipment to the value of £250,000.

Alongside qualifications in engineering and product design, 14–16-year-olds study GCSEs in English, maths, science and ICT, along with employability and enterprise skills. They also study German for engineering: indeed the teachers were so committed that they decided to learn it, too!

The same specialist subjects are available post-16, alongside A-levels including English, maths and science.

Students at the Black Country UTC benefit from an inspirational learning environment which replicates industry standards and is endorsed by international, national and local employers – over 40 companies in all. Five fully equipped engineering workshops are used for work on projects, and there are six science laboratories, a learning resource area and specialist ICT facilities throughout the building. Interactive technologies are at the heart of the learning, with a 1:1 ratio of ICT machines, a VLE (Virtual Learning Environment) and a wireless network extending across the entire campus. The campus also has the benefit of a specialist sports hall, swimming pool, astroturf pitch, lake and outdoor education facilities.

The UTC operates a significantly longer school day and year than most secondary schools. This makes it possible to offer students a greater range of extended learning activities, including performing arts, volunteering, extended projects and sporting activities.

The general pathway: the Liberal Arts College

This pathway will be familiar to many, as it is based on the existing GCSE/A-level route taken by young people who enjoy academic styles of learning. They are curious about facts, figures and ideas. They read and write fluently, quickly grasp complex concepts and have an ability to synthesize their thoughts both orally and in writing. Their parents and teachers may expect them to progress directly to full-time degree programmes soon after leaving school.

Because this style of education is so familiar, there is no real need to describe it in detail. However, I need to make an important point.

University of Exeter research for the Edge Foundation shows that 'academically able' young people enjoy and do well in practical subjects. Accordingly, the general pathway should not be based exclusively on learning by reading, writing and listening. Too often, young people are led to believe that success lies in writing the best essay, not in designing or making something tangible; something they can hold in their hands, or show with pride to their parents or future employers.

It is therefore vitally important that what many will describe as an 'academic' curriculum should be balanced by opportunities for creativity, including hands-on learning and a direct appreciation of technology. This could include working with wood, metal and plastic; it could also mean writing computer programs and creating apps for smartphones.

Equally, young people on this pathway should also gain experience of the world beyond the classroom, including learning about and through the world of work. Some schools think work-related learning is useful for pupils likely to enter the job market at 16 or 18, but not for those who plan to go straight to university. Yet, according to employers, many graduates leave HE inadequately prepared for the work. According to the CBI, 70 per cent of employers want university students to do more to prepare themselves to be effective in the workplace (2011, p. 6). However, there is much which schools – including Liberal Arts Colleges – can do, too, to prepare young people for work and help develop skills for adult life and employment.

In some rural areas, it may not be practical to offer a choice of four types of schools. There, the key will be to provide choices within a single school, or perhaps in schools which combine two or three pathways. This is what happened in the 1950s, when there were bilateral grammar and secondary modern schools, and even trilateral schools combining grammar, technical and modern streams in a single campus.

The case study offered here – Samuel Whitbread Academy – provides a model for this multilateral approach. It is a high school in a three-tier system, which offers both a stretching academic curriculum and a more focused technical programme. The thread which binds them together is engineering, offering challenge and context for young people of all talents and abilities.

Case study: Samuel Whitbread Academy

Picture 3.3 Samuel Whitbread Academy, Bedfordshire.

Samuel Whitbread Academy is a high school in rural Bedfordshire. Formerly a community college, it is a high school – or upper school – in a three-tier system, taking students from three middle schools at the age of 13.

The curriculum has been redesigned in recent years to make fuller use of the school's engineering specialism. In Key Stage 4 (age 13–16), students choose between a broad and focused route. The 'broad' curriculum offers a range of courses, including the most stretching and challenging academic subjects. The focused route enables students to spend one day a week studying either at Samuel Whitbread or at a partner college in subjects such as engineering, applied art and design, sport and ICT. All students study core subjects including English, maths and science, and the EBac – English, maths, science, a foreign language and either history or geography – is an option for all students, whether they choose the broad or focused route.

Similarly, post-16 students can choose traditional A-level subjects such as biology, chemistry, physics and French, alongside technical qualifications in engineering and ICT.

Senior leaders at Samuel Whitbread Academy are adamant that engineering must have an impact on the whole curriculum. Links with businesses have been especially effective, helping students learn through practical, real-world projects. In addition, it has helped students and parents appreciate that there are some cutting-edge businesses in the surrounding area – firms such as Lockheed Martin, a world-leading manufacturer of aeronautical and space systems. Another multinational business, SKF, helps students at Samuel Whitbread take part in Formula 24, a competition to design and race electric cars, and Vauxhall Motors gives graduate trainees time to visit the school to share their knowledge and experience.

The school has close ties with HE, too – not least, Cambridge University. Undergraduates act as e-mentors for Samuel Whitbread students, and also help with specific events such as a day spent designing and building model bridges. Although there was an emphasis on the practical skills involved in constructing bridges, much of the value lay in learning and applying mathematical concepts: one teacher described the event as a geometry day in disguise! This emphasis on teaching maths in context extends to post-16 students as well, and the school now offers a specific level 3 course in maths for engineers.

Similarly, links with both HE and employers have enabled the school to create hands-on projects which improve both written and spoken English.

The results have been impressive. On headline measures such as the achievement of five or more GCSE passes at grades A* to C, performance improved from 48 to 64 per cent in three years. At the same time, the sixth form has expanded dramatically: In 2012, the first year of sixth form will consist of 250 students moving up from Year 11, plus a number of students who have decided to transfer from other schools. As a result, it is now the largest sixth form in the local authority area.

Teachers are convinced that the curriculum offered by Samuel Whitbread Academy helps all students fulfil their potential. However, they also believe that being part of a three-tier system plays a part, too. They are convinced students benefit from the style of learning and pastoral support offered by middle schools, and arrive keen and ready for the style of learning offered by the Academy.

The sports and creative arts pathway: the Sports and Creative Arts College

Sports and Creative Arts Colleges will also provide a general education alongside specialisms from 14–19. They should be sponsored by a university and local or national employers.

The range of specialisms should cover the following:

- Sports, including sports science, physical education, event management and club management at national and local levels. Several sports could be offered by each college and it should be possible to cover all the main sports activities across the country.
- Performing arts, including theatre, dance, music – both classical and pop – theatre design and management, studio technology, recording and transmission and archive.

- Creative arts, including hand skills such as pottery, ceramics, textiles, sculpture, masonry, cabinet-making, bookbinding and photography.
- Fine arts, including drawing, painting and the history of art.

As with other pathways, there needs to be a significant element of learning by doing, as well as opportunities to develop wider skills for employment and adult life.

Case study: the BRIT School

Picture 3.4 The BRIT School, Croydon.

BRIT stands for the British Record Industry Trust, which sponsors the BRIT School, a specialist performing arts and technology school. When I was education secretary, I set in train the initial development of this school which has subsequently become a triumphant success.

The BRIT School is an independent, state-funded City College for the Technology of the Arts, the first of its kind in England to be dedicated to education and vocational training for the performing arts, media, art and design and the technologies that make performance possible.

As a school for 14–19-year-olds, the BRIT School is pioneering a new approach to education. It is not a stage or fame school, though most students intend to make a career in the arts, entertainment and communications industries.

The school also provides a general education to help young people prepare for the future. Students are encouraged to go on to specialist colleges and universities or into employment in the creative industries. Indeed, the majority do.

The focus of the school is on the arts and, where possible, National Curriculum subjects are linked to the arts via topics, projects or themes. State of the art resources mean students study in sophisticated environments equivalent to a modern workplace.

Students are admitted at 14 and 16. In Key Stage 4, there are approximately 170 pupils per year group; post-16, the number rises to 430.

The school recruits students who:

- aim for a life in the world of arts, entertainment and communication or related fields;

- demonstrate (with evidence) a commitment to the performing, visual or digital arts and their associated technologies, either in performance itself or in associated activities;

- demonstrate, during the application procedure, a real determination to study, practise and succeed;

- have the stamina and drive for the demanding schedule;

- demonstrate to the teachers they meet or work with during the application procedure that they would benefit from the education the BRIT School offers.

At Key Stage 4, students study English, maths, science, a modern foreign language, history or sociology (including religious studies) and physical education. Students also study for a BTEC Level 2 Diploma in a performing arts subject, broadcast and digital communication, visual arts and design or creative design and technology. Technology and ICT are taught within this course. Students choose one further subject from a list of options to broaden their learning.

Post-16, all students follow a Level 3, two-year programme leading to a BTEC Level 3 Extended Diploma. They also take additional courses to support the delivery of a broad and balanced curriculum. The majority of these are A-level courses.

More than two-thirds of the students who leave the BRIT School go into entertainment, music and media industry employment and courses. Some become professional actors, dancers and musicians. Others become stage managers or work for film and record companies. This list is by no means exhaustive – other opportunities include working in recording studios, operating cameras, song writing, arts administration, web design and teaching. Since 2011, the BRIT School has also offered a Foundation Degree in Digital Media Practice to students aged 18+, in partnership with Bournemouth University.

The school is very proud of the number of successful mainstream performers who studied there: between them, students have sold more than 63 million discs.

The career pathway: the Career College

This pathway will provide the general education which is common to all post-14 colleges, and will also provide vocational training in a range of subjects – for example, catering, hospitality, computing, security industry, fashion and textiles, hair and beauty, and the technical aspects of construction, plumbing, electrical work and building management.

In other words, students will be able to develop skills for specific occupations from the age of 14 onwards. This is a popular choice in Germany, Switzerland and Austria. It has also been tried before in this country – very successfully, as it happens.

Young Apprenticeships (YAs) were developed to offer motivated pupils aged 14–16 the opportunity to take industry-specific vocational qualifications alongside their programme of GCSEs. Typically, young people spent three days in school, one day at an FE college and one day in a workplace.

YAs proved popular and successful. They provided stretching, rigorous and enjoyable opportunities for young people to combine work-based learning with the core curriculum. Ofsted reported on them in glowing terms, commenting particularly on the motivation and enthusiasm of young apprentices and their high levels of achievement.

Numbers were always capped: no more than 10,000 young people were able to start a YA in any year. This meant there was never any opportunity for economies of scale. If only a handful of students at a particular school chose a YA, their school still had to employ a full complement of teaching and support staff. Furthermore, the school had to arrange special timetables so that students could fit their National Curriculum studies into just three days a week, which caused significant practical problems.

Following the Wolf Report on Vocational Education, the government announced that YAs would end, saying the high delivery costs could not be justified in the prevailing economic climate.

Career Colleges would be in a much better position than standard comprehensive schools to offer a new version of the YA. Every pre-16 student would be working away from the College for at least one day a week and staffing structures could be adjusted accordingly.

Once students achieve a full level 2 qualification – usually by the age of 16 or 17 – they would be given the opportunity to progress to a full level 3 qualification at the Career College or via an advanced apprenticeship. Much more of the post-16 study would be based in the student's workplace, with off-the-job training and development taking place in the college. Importantly, post-16 students would receive a wage from their employers.

As for progression to university, we already know that vocational qualifications can lead to HE, provided the quality is high enough, and provided admissions tutors look beyond their personal experience of GCSEs and A-levels to recognize the value of high-quality technical and vocational qualifications. Extra help may be required in specific areas such as essay writing and research skills, but Career Colleges would be well placed to provide this additional preparation for HE.

Another type of school which provides education and training at 14 – the Studio School – has also started up in England. It will be interesting to see how they develop, as they could provide a basis for Career Colleges.

Studio Schools are 14–18 schools, and generally support around 300 students. With year-round opening and a 9–5 working day, they feel more like a workplace than a school. Working closely with local employers, Studio Schools offer a range of academic and vocational qualifications including GCSEs in English, maths and science, as well as paid work placements linked directly to employment opportunities in the local area. National Curriculum subjects are delivered principally through working on enterprise projects at school, with local businesses and in the surrounding community.

It would also be possible for FE colleges to provide Career Colleges on or close to their own premises. They would have to be essentially self-contained institutions: some facilities could be shared but this should not diminish their separate status. Some FE colleges are already providing sites and premises to establish separate UTCs and this, too, could be a model for Career Colleges.

No doubt some people will criticize the idea of a distinct career pathway. Surely it will become the dumping ground for young people unable to do well in academic subjects? Surely it goes against the aspiration that more people from deprived neighbourhoods will find places at university?

On the contrary, I firmly believe that the vocational pathway could be every bit as successful as its equivalent in Germany and Austria, which provide excellent pathways to good qualifications, careers and – increasingly – HE. We can learn from them, just as we can learn from the American Career and Technical High Schools.

Case study: American Career and Technical High Schools

Career and Technical High Schools have been introduced in the past five years in certain American cities. I have visited two, the Food and Finance High School in midtown Manhattan and the Chelsea Career and Technical Education (CTE) High School. These start at 14 and continue on to 18 and 19.

In their own words, the Food and Finance High School is –

> . . . a small learning community with a focus on culinary arts. Our students take the full range of academic courses as well as a three year sequence in cooking and baking so that they graduate with both Regents Diploma and Food Industry Certifications. Students begin cooking in their Freshman year and by their senior year are placed in paid, work-based learning internships.
>
> Our community partner, Cornell University, brings us cutting edge scientific education through which our students raise fish in our aqua-culture lab and grow fresh produce in their science classes through the use of hydroponics. Other school partners bring health workshops and theater to our classroom.
>
> After school, our students can participate in nutrition education workshops, college courses, art club, step team, student government, extracurricular cooking and catering opportunities, and a full range of sports teams. We are in the process of expanding our catering business and developing additional student businesses.

The Food and Finance High School is rightly proud that former students have been admitted to a growing number of universities, showing that CTE can be a recognized route to HE as well as well-paid jobs and successful careers.

It is interesting, too, that this school occupies the site of a failed comprehensive. The school was closed and reopened as two separate institutions: one is the Food and Finance High School and the second is the High School for Hospitality Management. The only services they share are the sports hall and the canteen. Food and Finance High School has become very popular and is oversubscribed.

4

THE QUALIFICATIONS

Mike Tomlinson

Mention the words 'qualifications' or 'standards', and an argument and strong opinions are likely to follow.

For some, only GCSEs and A-level qualifications are worthy of mention, any others (if known at all) being regarded as options only for students who cannot manage 'academic' courses.

Increasingly, however, questions are being raised about both GCSE and A-level courses and qualifications. Some feel the demands made of students have declined, leading to lower standards over time. Others consider the knowledge base has been reduced. Yet others regard GCSEs as a poor basis for A-level study, which in turn is a poor basis for HE.

There have been many initiatives aimed at providing high-quality vocational/technical qualifications for 16-, 17- and 18-year-olds. A small number of these qualifications have proved their value over time to both employers and HE and have survived the many changes in the policies of successive governments. However, it remains the case that within England we do not have clear vocational routes populated with high-quality, rigorous courses credible with employers and parents. This is in stark contrast to the position in many of our European neighbours and, indeed, further afield.

Some history

Why are we in this position? Why is there continual tinkering with qualifications or the introduction of new ones?

A brief look back in history might provide some clues. From 1918 to 1951, the only qualifications available in England were the School Certificate and Higher School Certificate, the former awarded at 16 and the latter at 18. To achieve the School Certificate the student had to gain passes in English and mathematics and a number of other subjects from a prescribed list. (The EBac, introduced by Michael Gove in 2010, is based on a very similar list.) The Higher School Certificate at 18 was primarily a matriculation requirement for entry to HE: its make-up was determined by HE, related to particular degree courses. However, the vast majority of students left school at 14 and hence were never able to achieve any qualifications during their time in compulsory education.

The 1944 Education Act raised the school leaving age to 15 and introduced the tripartite system of grammar, technical and secondary modern schools. By 1951, the two school certificates had been replaced with O- and A-levels, each subject being separately qualified and graded. Initially, these qualifications were only available to students in selective grammar and technical schools, with secondary modern schools not being allowed to offer any formal qualifications.

In 1965 the Certificate of Secondary Education (CSE) was introduced, awarded by 14 new, separate awarding bodies. As O- and A-levels were primarily for students in selective schools (about 25% of the population), the CSE provided a qualification at 16 for the rest. Even then, not all eligible students in secondary modern schools – or the comprehensive schools which replaced them – took CSEs. To link the two systems, a Grade 1 at CSE was equated to a 'pass' at O-level. Very few people, least of all employers, ever believed this equivalence.

The introduction of A-levels heralded a post-16 curriculum which was highly specialized, academic and seen by some as narrow. Almost from the time of its introduction various concerns were expressed. Some objections related to the early specialization and others to more intriguing concerns, some of which affected O-levels as well.

For example, a Merseyside headmaster questioned the different proportions of students gaining a 'pass' in English via different examination boards, arguing that there should be 'some measure of national standard': the norm referencing of marks to determine grades. He argued that 'every school has its fat years and its lean years. And so have various subjects', and concluded by saying that the Fellowship of Independent Schools intended to introduce an examination of their own based on the old School Certificate (*Liverpool Daily Post*, 8 July 1952).

A second article was headed 'The General Certificate Rivals the Derby for Uncertain Results' (*Daily Mail*, 2 July 1952). Criticizing the new O-levels, a headmaster states: 'no one knows what standard is required to pass, or what exactly he will gain if he does pass.' He goes on to criticize the decision that O-levels can only be awarded to 16-year-olds (and no one younger) and complains about the fact that while 'the Durham examiners passed 86.5% in English language, the Joint [Matriculation] Board let through only 57.9%.'

Concerns with early specialization at A-level led to the establishment of the Crowther Committee in 1956, barely five years after the first A-level certificates were awarded. The final report defended early specialization while acknowledging the broader curricula followed in many other countries, but oddly stated:

> If a boy turns that intellectual corner, as he often does at the end of his Sixth Form time, we can be sure that, narrow as his education may have been during the last few years, he will take steps to widen it as well as deepen it. (Ministry of Education, 1959, p. 263)

To this day, many commentators find these conclusions rather inconsistent and opaque. Nevertheless, A-levels became well established, valued for entry to HE and regarded as the 'gold standard' qualification. This belief underpinned a continuing refusal by successive governments to countenance any radical revision of A-levels.

In 1972 the school leaving age was raised to 16. Post-16 staying-on rates have continued to rise since then. In 1976 only a quarter of 16- and 17-year-olds were in full-time education; by 1990 this had gone up to 39 per cent and by 2011 it was nearly 81 per cent (derived from Department for Education Statistical First Release 15/2011). The number of A-level entries has increased over time, too: in the 15 years from 1996 to 2011, entries rose from 620,000 to over 780,000, and the pass rate (A* to E) rose from 85.6 to 98.5 per cent (Department for Education Statistical First Release 01/2012).

Vocational qualifications

From 1976 onwards, various initiatives aimed to introduce vocational courses as alternatives to O- and A-levels. These were a response to the increasing post-16 staying-on rate, the need for qualifications for a growing number of students for whom O- and A-levels were inappropriate and as a consequence of increasing levels of youth unemployment in the late 1970s and early 1980s.

The many new initiatives and associated qualifications are too numerous to detail here, but a few are worthy of mention. The first, introduced from 1984, were pre-vocational qualifications: the Certificate of Extended Education (CEE), the Certificate of Pre-Vocational Education (CPVE) and City and Guilds 365. Second, National Vocational Qualifications (NVQs) were introduced after the National Council for Vocational Education was established in 1986. Intended primarily as qualifications to be gained on the job, NVQs rapidly came to be used to support full-time courses in FE colleges. Indeed, some NVQ units were used by schools for 14–19-year-olds. NVQs were followed by General National Vocational Qualifications (GNVQs), vocational GCSEs and vocational A-levels, and more recently Diplomas covering 14 vocational pathways.

While all these developments had the effect of establishing vocational pathways to complement the academic ones, they have not in total amounted to a coherent system, offering rigorous, high-quality vocational/technical pathways and qualifications understood and valued by employers, parents and HE. This remains the challenge today. Instead, we have thousands of individual courses and qualifications, many of which are poorly understood by parents and employers, many lacking in a strong general education component and their value in many cases remaining doubtful.

The Wolf Report on Vocational Education (2011) proposed a substantial reduction in the number of qualifications available to young people and set out criteria which those remaining should satisfy. While these changes are welcome in part, they still do not provide the high-quality vocational/technical pathways so urgently needed.

GCSEs and A-levels

The first General Certificate of Secondary Education (GCSE) examinations were taken in 1988. This development was probably the most significant change to the qualification system since 1951. The new qualification, introduced by Sir Keith Joseph, replaced both O-levels and CSEs with a single system. Sir Keith claimed that the new qualification would be 'tougher, but clearer and fairer' (Hansard HC 20 June 1984, vol. 62, c. 306).

At the same time, the former CSE and O-level awarding bodies began a process of combination which today has given us four main awarding bodies in England and one each in Wales and Northern Ireland. Each offers qualifications at GCSE and A-level, alongside a range of vocational qualifications. (Scotland, on the other hand, has always had its own education and qualifications systems.)

Meanwhile, concerns with A-levels continued, mostly centred on the recurring argument about early specialization. Successive reports including Ron Dearing's Review of Qualifications for 16–19 year olds (1996) and the Tomlinson Report (2004) argued for a broader post-16 curriculum, high-quality vocational provision and some form of diploma to match the much admired International Baccalaureate (IB). All foundered to a greater or lesser extent on the determination of successive governments to defend and retain the 'gold standard' A-level qualification.

Changes were eventually made as a result of the introduction of Curriculum 2000, which introduced the Advanced Supplementary (AS) qualification, a half-way house between GCSE and the full A-level. Other adjustments included the introduction of an A* grade, the modularization of A-levels (and later GCSEs) and a reduction in the volume of coursework. Despite everything, the volume of criticism of both GCSEs and A-levels did not diminish. Furthermore, a growing number of independent schools – and some state schools too – adopted the International GCSE (IGCSE), which is more like the old O-level, and replaced A-levels with the IB.

Continuing challenges in an incoherent system

Despite multiple initiatives and reforms, we still do not have a coherent system of qualifications offering students clear progression routes to HE or employment. Instead, piecemeal changes have created a hotchpotch of qualifications which, at least in part, are not well understood by parents, teachers, employers or HE. A strong vocational/technical pathway remains elusive given the strong pressure to focus on 'academic' achievement far more than technical excellence. GCSEs and A-levels have seen their knowledge requirement reduced and assessments fail to differentiate well enough between the performance of the more able students and reward scholarship.

Although many people leap to the defence of the present qualification system, the fact remains it is not fit for purpose in the twenty-first century. Employers continue to complain about the levels of numeracy and literacy associated with GCSE grades. HE complains about the failure of A-levels to develop research skills or promote independent learning. There is general concern about the quality of technical education and the supply of well-educated technicians.

There are some exceptions within the present system but they cannot hide the weaknesses, nor answer the fundamental questions to be asked of our qualifications. Are they fit for purpose? Do they tell us what we want to know? Is narrow post-16 specialization any longer sensible, given all the uncertainties in today's employment world? Should we move away from examinations at a specified age to taking them when young people are ready for them? Do the curriculum and its associated qualifications equip today's young people with the knowledge, personal qualities and skills needed to be successful in the fast-changing economic and social environment?

What is not in doubt is that GCSEs and AS/A-levels exert a disproportionate influence not only over what is taught in English secondary schools but also on *how* it is taught. Teaching to the test has become the norm and the high stakes associated with the results every year for the student, the school and the system as a whole have come to dominate all debate about education in England. In addition, a vast amount of teaching time is taken up by examinations and the cost to schools and colleges is enormous. As to the former, it is estimated that examinations taken by 14–19-year-olds take up one whole term of teaching time, while the cost of entry fees has increased dramatically to around £150,000 per annum for a comprehensive school and about £300,000 per annum for a college. Both of these demands by the examination system need to be reduced.

We also need to examine the interesting question of grade inflation: that is, the continued increase in the proportion of students gaining both a pass grade and A*/A grades. The steady rise over time has led to charges of 'dumbing down'.

While it has become commonplace to accept allegations of grade inflation, a report published by the OECD in 2003 stated that *every* significant industrialized country had recorded sharp increases in the number of students passing their school leaving examinations over the past four decades. Analysis of the academic record of people in different age bands showed that 55 per cent of Britons aged between 55 and 64 had (at that time) at least five O-levels or GCSEs at grades A to C. This figure rose to 68 per cent for those aged between 25 and 34. In France the equivalent figures were 46 per cent for older adults and 78 per cent for younger adults; in Australia 44 per cent and 71 per cent; and in Japan 63 per cent and 94 per cent. The report's author, Andreas Schleicher, argued that the trend was driven by the same economic factor – the importance attached to qualifications as governments seek greater economic growth ('Exam grade rises "not confined to British students"', *The Times*, 18 August 2003).

It is unlikely that an international conspiracy has been hatched to increase the proportion gaining the qualifications through grade inflation. It is much more likely that the changes, at least in part, are a result of improvements in teaching and the hard work of students.

Four questions

In considering what should be done to reform our qualifications system, some account has to be taken of the review of the National Curriculum initiated by the coalition government, the decision to raise the education leaving age to 17 in 2013 and to 18 in 2015 and the emergence of new types of 14–19 schools – particularly UTCs.

Let us assume we have three qualification pathways available to students from the age of 14: the so-called academic pathway hitherto dominated by GCSEs and A-levels; the vocational/technical pathway; and the apprenticeship route. (The four 14–18 colleges proposed by Kenneth Baker would of course offer a range of qualifications.)

Four questions deserve consideration. The first relates to the National Curriculum, which currently dictates what is taught in schools up to the age of 16 (end of Key Stage 4). Is it time to have the National Curriculum end at the age of 14 (end of Key Stage 3), with only the core subjects of English, mathematics and science being compulsory in Key Stage 4?

The second question concerns the place of GCSEs as a 'school leaving' examination – which was its original purpose – when the education leaving age is being raised to 18 by 2015. Such a costly and all-consuming examination no longer appears as necessary or relevant as it once did. Could GCSEs be replaced by an assessment system which both reports on the progress being made by students and also on the level of attainment at 16 as part of a continuum of study from 14 to 18? This sort of information would enable teachers, students and parents to be sure the appropriate pathway was being followed and the expected progress being made towards a 'Graduation Certificate' available from 18 onwards.

Thirdly, responsibility for general qualifications (and most vocational ones, too), rests with just four awarding bodies in England. Is the time ripe to consider moving to a single national awarding body or some variant on this model?

Finally, should consideration be given to requiring all students to continue to study mathematics and English up to the age of 18, the content being chosen to support their main studies (assuming these do not include mathematics or English)? This is common in many countries and is a feature of the curriculum model being used by UTCs.

None of these questions has a simple answer, but if we are serious about having world-class qualifications and hence a world-class education system, they at least deserve debate.

The way ahead

More immediately, there are changes to the present qualifications which can and should be made:

1 Identify, with the help of employers, the literacy and numeracy knowledge and skills needed by school leavers at 16, 17 and 18 and incorporate these 'cores' into GCSE English and mathematics. The examination system should enable not only an overall grade to be given but also a grade for each of the 'cores'. Grades A* to C should not be awarded without a specified performance in the core. This should enable employers to know better the literacy and numeracy competency of young people and the results in the cores could become a key measure of the effectiveness of every school.

Picture 4.1 Science at the Black Country UTC, Walsall.

2 Increase the knowledge content of both GCSEs and A-levels to ensure easier progression from GCSE to A-level and from A-level to HE. In the case of A-levels, the HE sector should agree a common core of content which has to be included in each A-level course. This would also help progression and reduce the need for first year university courses to cover ground which should be contained within A-level programmes. In the case of the physical sciences and engineering courses at A-level, the quantitative content should be reinstated following its gradual reduction over recent years.

3 Ensure the technical content of vocational courses is specified by employers, as it is in UTCs. Employers should also have a say in some of the teaching and learning approaches, such as group projects. Alongside this technical content there should be a strong general education element, which is characteristic of vocational courses in other countries and of the new International Baccalaureate Career-Related Certificate (IBCC). These steps should ensure there are high-quality, rigorous vocational pathways with inbuilt progression and coherence. Only institutions with teachers experienced in the vocational area being taught, with facilities and equipment which reflect current practice in employment and structured exposure of students to the workplace, should be allowed to offer vocational courses – in effect, accredited providers.

4 Ensure assessment methods used within qualifications support the curriculum and its desired outcomes and do not, as at present, dictate pedagogy. Greater use of extended writing and synoptic questions is needed to replace much of the dull questioning now seen. Examination papers should encourage and reward students' passion for, and knowledge of, their subject, whether academic or vocational. Where appropriate, students' practical skills should be assessed as well as their subject knowledge.

5 Abandon modular structures for examinations in favour of a terminal assessment which is taken when the student is ready – whether at 15, 16, 17 or 18. The AS qualification should be retained to encourage both breadth and progression post-16.

6 Move to have only one awarding body responsible for examining at GCSE each of the subjects in the National

Curriculum. The award of such a contract would also include a requirement to continue to provide for minority subjects. Through this mechanism the best examiners and markers would come together under one awarding body, standards could be more clearly stated and monitored over time and it would remove competition which revolves largely around assessment demands.

7 Seek ways of providing the apprenticeship route with an overall qualification. This may require greater commonality of approaches and demands across sectors, but it would add to the value of this important route.

8 Periodically review and recalibrate the standards associated with specific qualifications, taking account of international trends. In every Olympic year the qualifying performance for each sport is reviewed and may be raised in comparison with the previous games. This in no way reduces the value of the gold medal awarded in previous games, but it is unlikely a past winner would qualify for the final in – say – 2020. In the same way, the demands on students may need to increase over time, even if this leads to fewer students gaining a pass grade.

This is a challenging list of changes to consider. However, concerns with our qualification system are now such that simple tinkering is unlikely to solve some deep-rooted problems. Changes are now needed both to the system as a whole and to individual qualifications. We cannot have an internationally high-quality education system without an equivalent qualification system. This we do not have at present, most notably with regard to the vocational/technical pathway.

This leads to one further consideration. An issue which is common to all routes is the need to develop and recognize skills which are not subject specific. These include the capacity to work in a team, the management of time and their own work, research skills, problem-solving skills and presentational, including oral, skills. These skills and attributes are valuable in themselves, but also for progression to further learning and work.

Many other countries tackle this by having a baccalaureate structure which recognizes achievement in a range of subjects and skills. Within the United Kingdom, the Welsh Baccalaureate recognizes achievement in GCSEs, A-levels, vocational qualifications and a common core comprising humanities, personal and social education, work-related learning, numeracy and literacy skills and an individual project or investigation. The IB – which, as noted above, is offered by some schools in England – embraces subject learning, an extended essay, the theory of knowledge, creativity, action and community service. A number of countries also have high school graduation certificates or diplomas: for example, the Ontario Secondary School Diploma is awarded to students who achieve credits in a blend of compulsory and optional subjects taught between the ages of 14 and 18, some of which may be technical and vocational.

Of course, this is not the first time a baccalaureate structure has been proposed in England. I had the pleasure and privilege to chair a Working Group on 14–19 Reform established by the Labour government in 2003. We consulted a great number of people over the following 18 months before presenting our final report to the then–Secretary of State Charles Clarke (Department for Education and Skills, 2004). We concluded that all 14–19-year-olds should have access to coherent and relevant learning programmes comprising the following:

- core learning, which is about getting the basics right and developing the generic knowledge, skills and attributes necessary for participation in HE, working life and the community; and

- main learning chosen by the learner to develop knowledge, skills and understanding of academic and vocational subjects and disciplines which provide a basis for work-based training, HE and employment.

We went on to describe how achievement should be recognized by new diplomas at four levels – Entry, Foundation, Intermediate and Advanced. Diploma transcripts would provide easily accessible information about the grades contributing to each student's diploma, as well as other achievements in wider activities. As we conceived them, diplomas were a baccalaureate in all but name.

As with previous attempts at reform, the Working Group's proposals foundered largely because the government chose to defend and retain 'gold standard' A-levels. Instead, the government concluded that a new suite of Diplomas should be offered *alongside* GCSEs and-A levels.

The idea of an overarching framework proved attractive to the eminent educationalists who conducted the Nuffield Review of 14–19 Education and Training, a remarkable five-year programme of research and debate which culminated in 2009 with the publication of *Education for All: The Future of Education and Training for 14–19 Year Olds*. The review concluded – among other things – that England needs a baccalaureate-type curriculum and qualifications framework. The review suggested that achievements in academic, technical and vocational subjects should be incorporated into an overall framework balancing theoretical and applied learning, subject knowledge and skills and broader competences such as problem-solving (Pring et al., 2009).

The 2010 General Election ushered in a coalition government. The new Secretary of State for Education, Michael Gove, took steps to make GCSEs and A-levels more rigorous, and invited Professor Alison Wolf to conduct a review of vocational education for 14–19-year-olds. He also announced an EBac, with the explicit aim of encouraging more young people to take a particular combination of subjects during Key Stage 4: English, maths, science, a foreign language (ancient or modern) and either history or geography. This is a baccalaureate in the sense that it recognizes achievement across several subjects, but it is limited to Key Stage 4 and does not recognize success in technical or vocational subjects, or wider achievements in problem-solving, teamwork and other skills desired by employers and HE alike.

I remain convinced that we need a baccalaureate in the wider sense of the term. Recognizing that the education leaving age is rising to 18, however, the focus should no longer be on achievement at 16. Instead, I agree with Kenneth Baker that we should regard the years from 14 to 18 as a single phase of education, leading to a Graduation Certificate at 18+. The Graduation Certificate should be awarded to anyone who reaches a specified level in their academic, technical/vocational and apprenticeship studies, including the broader skills needed for success in further learning, work and adult life.

There will still be a need to track individual student's progress. Many will still take tests and exams at 16, and they will still choose to specialize in a smaller number of subjects at 17 and 18.

However, 16 should no longer be seen as a concrete dividing line between one stage of learning and another, or between one type of qualification and another. The Graduation Certificate should become the end point for all young people, summing up and recognizing all that they have learned and achieved by the age of 18 (or over), including individual elements completed at 16, 17 or 18.

5
MAKING 14–18 EDUCATION A REALITY

Alan Smithers

Education in England lacks a clear shape. Nowhere is this more apparent than in the final years of secondary schooling. In this chapter I will argue that raising the participation age to 18 in England – legislated by the previous government and accepted by the Coalition elected in 2010 – means that a school leaving examination at age 16 is no longer needed. Dropping or moving the current examinations, the GCSE and equivalents, and treating education 14–18 as a whole would open up the opportunity to create a coherent array of routes to university, further training, employment and future lives.

Current assortment

Depending on where young people of secondary school age live and what their parents know about education provision, they could find themselves in a school with a leaving age of 16, one that runs through to 18, a sixth-form college, a tertiary college or an FE college. The school could have a subject label which might or might not indicate its strengths (Smithers and Robinson, 2009); it could be a grammar school which selected at age 11; it could be a comprehensive admitting across the range or one which partly selected on ability or was socially skewed by its locality or religious affiliation; or it could be a secondary modern school for those not getting into grammar schools; and there are a handful of technical schools and city technology colleges. Many schools are currently converting to academies which will have greater freedom than those remaining in local authorities. 'Free' schools are also being added to the mix.

The school or college might provide very good academic courses favoured by top universities (Russell Group, 2011), or offer and encourage seemingly equivalent GCSEs and A-levels that are not acceptable. There might be very good vocational courses that feed into apprenticeships and employment, or courses that purport to be vocational but which are to all intents and purposes worthless when students seek to move on to other courses or into the workplace.

The courses and qualifications offered by a school or college could be influenced as much by league table points as by the likely benefits to pupils.

At present, compulsory schooling ends at age 16. But from 2013 everyone will be required to stay in education and training till the age of 17, and from 2015 to the age of 18. Given that this major change is just around the corner you might have thought that a clear pattern of provision was emerging. The term '14–19' is increasingly being used, which suggests that it is to be a stage in its own right, but so far it has little basis in reality. Furthermore, the label is unhelpful in that it implies a period of five years whereas, in fact, it is just four – Years 10 to 13 in current parlance. Here '14–18' is preferred.

The split at age 16

The present government has been, nevertheless, far from idle when it comes to the final years of secondary education. But the signs are that it has decided to continue with a sharp split at the current school leaving age. Its main accountability measure will continue for the present to be based on GCSEs at age 16. Any school not reaching a floor standard for 16-year-olds faces being closed or taken over.[1] It has also been devising a range of performance measures[2] for schools at age 16, including one, the EBac, which might lead to the award of a certificate. This requires pupils to have passed six GCSEs in specified subjects (English, maths, science, a foreign language and either history or geography) at least at grade C and is designed to drive schools into concentrating on academic subjects.

Rather surprisingly, this academic focus has received support from the Wolf Review of Vocational Education. Professor Wolf heavily criticized the vocational qualifications currently available at Key Stage 4, and recommended a core academic curriculum pre-16, postponing vocational specialization to post-16 (2011, p. 11). The split at 16 has also been underlined by the withdrawal from January 2011 of the funding for the YA programmes, which enabled 14–16-year-olds to take industry-specific or vocationally related qualifications alongside GCSEs. Post-16 apprenticeships, however, will continue to be funded.

Arguments for a split at age 16

Underlying the 14–16/16–18 split seems to be the belief that academic courses open up opportunities but vocational courses restrict them. Nick Gibb, the schools minister, said in evidence to the House of Commons Education Committee that the EBac, 'is about delaying specialisation until 16 and keeping options open as long as possible, so that people are not closing down opportunities post-16' (House of Commons Education Committee, 2011, Q125). Two other objections to clear routes at Key Stage 4 are that 14-year-olds lack the maturity to take crucial decisions about subjects and fields, and that any major shift in the pattern of provision 14–18 would involve a considerable upheaval in institutional arrangements.

Although plausible none of these arguments is conclusive. Take the sweeping generalization that academic courses keep options open and vocational courses close them down. While it is true that vocational courses by definition have a specific purpose, it is good courses of whatever stripe that enhance opportunities and poor courses that restrict them. The HE white paper recognizes, for example, that not all A-levels are acceptable to the top universities and welcomes the Russell Group's advice on 'facilitating' subjects (Department for Business, Innovation and Skills, 2011, p. 31).

For her part, Professor Wolf appears to object to vocational education pre-16 because she could not find evidence that it led to improvements in general attainment (2011, p. 109). But she seems to have missed the important research of Sig Prais and his team at the National Institute for Economic and Social Research in the 1980s and 1990s, which showed that good vocational education opened up opportunities by providing the incentive for the more practically inclined to get to grips with a core of essential education. Prais found, for example, that 70 per cent of pupils on pre-16 vocational courses in Germany could divide $18^3/_5$ by $7^3/_4$ whereas only 10 per cent of pupils of similar age and ability in England but on academic courses could do the easier $1^1/_3$ divided by $^8/_9$. Even with more able pupils included only 40 per cent could do it (Prais et al., 1991, pp. 21–2).

Wolf seems to be confusing the quality of what is currently on offer with what it could be. She and the government are surely right to recognize that there is a core of essential learning, but wrong to think that this is better provided for all young people through academic courses than to have the option of pursuing it through a vocational programme.

As regards the second objection, lengthening compulsory education does extend childhood and dependency. But this does not mean that young people are biologically incapable of taking important decisions. When compulsory education ended earlier than it does now, young people showed themselves perfectly capable of getting on with their lives (Musgrove, 1964, pp. 33–57 and 155–6). If the assumption now is that young people do not know what they are good at, what they like and what they want to do after nine years of required school attendance, then the quality of that education has to be questioned.

Truancy increases fivefold from Years 7 to 11, as more and more children decide that school is not for them (Department for Education Statistical First Release 03/2011). Other children continue to show up, but express their dissatisfaction through being disruptive. Choices at 14 would restore to young people some control over their lives, and mean that potential truants could take decisions within education instead of, as now, *in extremis* having to go outside it.

On the third objection, it may seem practical politics to stay with the education stages we now have rather than getting involved in the upheaval and expense of new institutional structures. But the upheaval may be less than supposed and change could be allowed to emerge rather than being imposed. Most secondary schools do run either from 11 to 16 or 11 to 18, but there are also types of school and college with starting ages of 9, 10, 12, 13, 14 and 16. In some local authorities there are middle schools followed by high schools to which there may or may not be automatic transfer. Some of the new academies run all through from primary to secondary. There would be no need for the wholesale imposition of a new structure from the centre. There could be incentives for schools to adapt to a new pattern which would emerge over time.

Experience elsewhere

What is striking about the organization of education in England compared with that in other countries is the lack of clear routes in the final years of secondary schooling. There is a strong ladder to university through GCSEs and A-levels but off that ladder young people have to find their way through a maze of qualifications of uncertain value. Many of the offerings smack of finding something to do for the less academically able rather than being genuinely about enhancing lives. In contrast, in 26 states which were members of the Organisation of Economic and Cultural Development (OECD) in 2006, there are clearly signposted academic, practical and work-related routes (Smithers and Robinson, 2010, p. 25).

These are accommodated within different structures in different ways. In some countries, for example, Germany and the Netherlands, there are different types of secondary school for the different routes. In others, including France and Japan, there are intermediate (what we would call middle) schools followed by high schools containing the different routes. The Nordic pattern is for all-ability schools to run through the years of compulsory schooling from age 6 or 7 to 16. Pupils can then opt to continue in high schools (it is not compulsory, but participation exceeds 90%) where there are different routes as in Finland or with different lines within the same school as in Sweden. In yet other countries, including Belgium and Italy, education is organized as a sequence of cycles with the different routes opening up in one of the cycles – in Belgium, for example, education from age 14 takes four forms: general, technical, artistic and vocational. But whatever the pattern there are clear routes through for everyone. The only exceptions, beside England, are the United States and Canada which seek (very largely) to defer vocational education to post-school provision, and New Zealand which has options within a common qualifications framework.

The OECD draws together these different systems of school organization by distinguishing lower secondary education from upper secondary education. Lower secondary is defined as the three years after primary education, and upper secondary as the formal education and training which follows. These terms, commonplace in other countries, are alien to English ears because the distinction is not recognized. England de facto has a period of general lower secondary education lasting five years with upper secondary education compressed into two.

The Wolf Report claims that transition at age 16 is the norm in Europe (2011, p. 42). But this ignores the later starting of formal education in several of those countries. If formal education does not begin till age 6 or 7 then nine years of primary and lower secondary education is not completed till the age of 15 or 16. There then usually follow three or four years of upper secondary education or training rather than just two as in England.

Upper secondary education is not compulsory in 19 (current) OECD member states. Nevertheless in 10 of the 19 there was over 90 per cent participation, which suggests that provision is highly regarded and of good quality. Access to the different routes is a choice-eligibility process. Teachers provide guidance (often based on tests or formal assessment[3]), but parental choice is paramount.

According to figures published by the OECD in 2009, overall just over half of all young people choose academic routes (54%) and just under half vocational routes (46%) (table C1.1, p. 304). Significantly, England was unable to provide accurate data. About a third of those on vocational routes (14 of the 46 percentage points) were in a mix of school- and work-based settings. This is the major vocational route in Switzerland, Denmark and Germany. Employers were also prominently involved in the design of vocational awards in other countries.

Differentiation in education

England seems to have been so scarred by its experience of the 11+ examination that it seems unwilling to contemplate any overt differentiation in education. There is much wishful thinking. Those who claim that hard work is much more important than talent have popular appeal.[4] They appear to promise that you can do anything provided you put in the hours of practice. There is differentiation of sorts in schools – tiers, sets and streams – but it is not to be spoken about. The various attempts to provide for the gifted and talented have foundered because many schools have been unwilling to identify pupils as such (Smithers and Robinson, 2011). At the other end of the scale, great store is set by inclusion irrespective of whether the pupil would benefit from special provision. And while it is accepted that pupils perform differently in tests and examinations and that prior attainment is the best predictor of future performance,[5] it is insisted that this implies individual personalized provision, not the grouping together of pupils of similar abilities and interests.

The 11+ examination was, in its time, the engine of social mobility. When grammar schools were at their height, Britain had the highest proportion of university students of working class origin in Western Europe (Shirley Williams, quoted in Flew, 1987, p. 30). Countless men and women from low-income homes have owed their professional elevation to their grammar school education. But it has become widely accepted that the price paid by those not selected at age 11 was too high. A great mistake, however, was made in not replacing the grammar schools with anything that served different abilities, interests and aspirations. Harold Wilson, prime minister of the government that did the most to dismantle the grammar schools, boasted that comprehensive schools would provide a grammar school education for everyone (Smithers and Robinson, 1991, p. 19). It was blithely assumed that everyone wanted and would benefit from academic study.

More recently, Alastair Campbell – Tony Blair's spokesman at 10 Downing Street – claimed that 'the day of the bog-standard comprehensive school is over' (TES, 16 February 2001). However, the Labour Party refused to contemplate any form of selection. Blair attempted to side-step the issue by adopting the mantra 'standards not structures' (Barber, 2007, p. 23), which begs the question, 'standards in what?' To move beyond comprehensive schools the Blair government promoted diversity, including schools that bore specialist subject labels, but were not able to recruit on talent for the subject, so adding to the confusion. Even worse, those more motivated by practical study or who wanted to get out into work were denied the opportunity to hone their skills, by the well-intentioned but misguided wish to protect them from discrimination.

The organization of education in other countries clearly demonstrates that differentiation does not have to be by selection and it does not have to be at age 11. In 1991, I was one of a commission of five educationists who were asked by Channel 4 Television to investigate the state of education in England (Prais et al., 1991). We sifted the evidence and visited schools in the Netherlands, Germany and France, as well as in England. We were charged with identifying important reforms that could be introduced in the short run, say 18 months, without absorbing undue additional resources. Although we came from across the political spectrum we found it remarkably easy to reach agreement.

Much of what we recommended has become or is becoming part of the education landscape, including putting English and arithmetic at the centre of primary education, external tests at the end of primary school, a national curriculum occupying no more than half to two-thirds of the timetable with the rest decided locally, examination standards to be regulated by a body set up for the purpose and the need to sharpen up vocational qualifications. But a key proposal – that there should be a choice of routes from the age of 14 – has still not found favour.

Routes from age 14

That the government is not entirely against differentiation at age 14 is suggested by its response to the Wolf Review when it says that it wishes to see more young people having the opportunity to switch to FE colleges before they reach the age of 16 (Department for Education, 2011c, p. 11).

As Kenneth Baker has outlined in earlier chapters, the 2011 budget set out a commitment to establish at least 24 new UTCs by 2014, and the Young Foundation, supported by the Edge Foundation, has formed the Studio Schools Trust (see Chapters 2 and 3).

UTCs and Studio Schools are only beginning to get under way, but they signal a growing recognition of 14 as the age of transfer. They join 108 maintained high schools which admit at ages 13 or 14, and the government is seeking to encourage enrolment pre-16 in FE colleges.

In the independent sector, 13 has long been the age of transfer to senior schools.

Advantages of differentiation at age 14

The advantages of treating 14–18 as an integral phase in education fall into three broad groups: enhancing people's lives, connecting with employment opportunities and giving shape to an inchoate education system.

The fundamental reason for different routes is that people do differ. It is reasonable to require all children to be at school and to follow the same core curriculum for some part of their lives so that they can learn to handle words and numbers, have the opportunity to experience the main ways of making sense of the world and learn to be responsible citizens. But if their education means anything at all they will be coming to know themselves. Once they are clearer about who they are, they will want to do different things. At some point, therefore, there has to be a shift from requiring young people to follow a common curriculum whether they want to or not, to providing an array of opportunities among which choices are made. As was realized with the 11+ test, the age of 11 is too early; 16 is too late because it leaves insufficient time for progression to the different destinations. And, as we have seen, those not served by the current undifferentiated offering vote with their feet in large numbers or become disruptive.

A second major reason is that the education system lacks proper connection with employment opportunities. This manifests itself in a number of ways. At a time when there has been an explosion in 'vocational' qualifications for 14–16-year-olds, employers have never been more vocal in complaining about the educational system (see, for example, CBI, 2010 and 2011). The explanation seems to be that employers have been little involved in the design of those qualifications and have little regard for them. The qualifications are mainly taught in schools as part of the general curriculum with little specialized equipment and by teachers with little direct experience of employment outside schools, which greatly restricts what can be offered. The courses are mainly an afterthought to the academic curriculum, not something designed in their own right. Establishing clear routes from 14 would provide the stimulus to create courses and awards with considerable input from employers so they would be happy to recruit on the qualifications and perhaps pay people more for having them.

Clear routes through upper secondary education would also enable the country to tackle the crucial shortage of technicians which is hampering developments in many fields, including nanotechnology, pharmaceuticals and medical science, renewable technologies, aerospace and aircraft maintenance, transportation, the nuclear industry and engineering of various kinds (Medhat, 2009). The shortages are currently being met mainly by immigration (ONS, July 2011); indeed, employment is the most important reported reason for immigration to the United Kingdom (Migration Watch, 12 August 2010). While politicians might urge UK businesses to give a chance to unemployed Britons rather than relying on foreign workers, employers retort that migrants often have better skills and a better work ethic.

In the first quarter of 2012, nearly one in ten (9.8%) of 16- to 18-year-olds was not in education, employment or training (NEET) (Department for Education Statistical Release May 2012). This is dispiriting enough, but there is evidence that it is associated with later negative outcomes such as poor health, psychological problems, poverty and criminal records (Department for Work and Pensions and Department for Education, 2011). Well-thought-out routes from the age of 14, as exemplified by UTCs, would do much to give young people a better platform for their future lives and help to redress the balance.

The third group of advantages centres on bringing coherence to what has become a disparate 'system'. In fact such has been the emphasis on individual schools that it hardly merits being called a system. We have already noted that education in other countries generally has a much clearer shape. In England the wide range of transition ages could come to coalesce around 14. Freely chosen routes at 14 would make sense of a specialist schools policy which leaves the schools unable to select on talent. Science schools in the United States, Japan and Korea point the way (Smithers and Robinson, 2009). Gifted and talented provision could be incorporated instead of it being a bolt-on. Distinctive qualifications would bring sharpness and precision to the little-understood National Qualifications Framework. An even more exciting prospect is that some of the former direct grant grammars, like Bradford and Manchester, that were forced to become independent by the Labour government of 1976 might rejoin the state sector if they were allowed to differentiate from the age of 14.[6]

Putting a shape on 14–18 education

What then should be done? In my view, it is this: create an array of interconnected equivalent routes leading to national qualifications in academic subjects, practical/technical subjects and occupational fields spanning the age range 14–18. The qualifications would have to be agreed with the potential end-users – the universities and employers – such that they would base recruitment decisions on them. Academic subject qualifications would be single subject qualifications and could derive from A-levels with more HE involvement; BTECs, diplomas and other vocational qualifications should be reformed in consultation with employers so that they become agreed programmes embracing core subjects and practical skills leading to recognized qualifications.

The routes would necessarily be of different lengths, so the government should think again about compelling participation to age 18. It has already delayed the enforcement procedures envisaged by the previous government. Only three countries in the OECD (the Netherlands, Hungary and some provinces of Canada) have full-time compulsory education and training to the age of 18, though three others (Belgium, Germany and Poland) require at least part-time attendance.

England should accept the OECD distinction between lower secondary education which has a compulsory common curriculum and upper secondary education which provides a range of opportunities. Applying the OECD definition would suggest 14 as the age of transfer. A qualification should mark the completion of lower secondary and be the basis for entry to the routes in upper secondary. That qualification could be the GCSE moved forward or an award derived from it.

The routes should be freely chosen by parents and pupils on the advice of teachers and a guidance service. Year 10 could be an orientation year in which decisions about routes could be tested out and minds changed. There would also be ample opportunities to move later between the routes, though switching might involve taking longer to reach certain qualifications.

Schools and colleges should be encouraged to adapt to the new pattern. There are already high schools in three-tier systems, UTCs and Studio Schools. FE colleges already have experience of taking pupils from the age of 14 and the government supports growth in this provision. Some 11–18 schools might wish to provide for 14–18 and some current 11–14 and 11–16 schools might wish to recruit from an earlier age. Senior independent schools joining the maintained sector would find it easy to provide for 14–18-year-olds.

My main message is that the education system must be given a clear shape so that all parents are able to find a good place for their children. Recent governments have concentrated on improving individual schools to the neglect of the overall framework. The picture I have in mind is of an oak tree with roots feeding into a trunk of a common curriculum which bears an array of strong branches. The branches could begin to form at age 11 or 16, but there is much to recommend age 14. With the raising of the participation age, the time has come to make education 14–18 a reality.

Notes

1   Currently the floor standard is 35% of pupils not reaching five GCSEs A*–C including English and maths and fewer pupils making progress between Key Stages 2 and 4 than the national average. In a speech to the National College for School Leadership on 16 June 2011 the secretary of state announced that the 'floor' will be raised to 50% by 2015.

2   A performance measure in the government's terminology differs from accountability measures in that it is designed to inform the public, not to trigger sanctions against schools. The issue was explored by the House of Commons Education Committee during oral evidence by the Minister of State for Schools, Nick Gibb, on 27 April 2011 (House of Commons Education Committee, 2011, Ev 18 onwards).

3   In 21 of the 26 countries there is formal assessment at the end of lower secondary education, in 8 involving external exams or a monitoring test, and in 13 internal assessment. In 5 countries pupils move forward within the different types of school they go to after primary (Smithers and Robinson, 2010, chart 5.3, p. 30).

4 For example, M. Syed (2011), *The Bounce*, London: Fourth Estate; G. Colvin (2008), *Talent Is Over-Rated*, London: Nicholas Brealey Publishing; D. Coyle (2010), *The Talent Code*, London: Arrow.

5 This is the assumption that underpins value added measures of school effectiveness: see, for example, the method of calculating the Key Stage 2 to Key Stage 4 value added measure, at www.education.gov.uk/performancetables/va1_03/docD.shtml

6 Personal communication from the head of a leading former direct grant school.

6

PATHWAYS, NOT TRACKS: AN AMERICAN PERSPECTIVE

Robert B. Schwartz

In February 2011, two colleagues – economist Ronald Ferguson and journalist William Symonds – and I released a report titled *Pathways to Prosperity* (Symonds et al., 2011).

When we first began meeting to discuss the study that led to this report, we were mindful that 20 years earlier a commission established by the W.T. Grant Foundation had issued a powerful report called *The Forgotten Half: Non-College Bound Youth in America* (Halperin, 1988). As the title suggests, this report argued that public resources and support were disproportionately focused on young people headed for HE, and that without a much more robust investment in preparing non-college-bound youth for successful transition into the workforce, these young people would be at significant social and economic risk. The jumping-off question for our study was: is there still a 'forgotten half' today, and, if so, how do we make more progress in serving that population in the next 20 years than we have made in the past 20?

On the face of it, it seemed unlikely that we would find a persisting 'forgotten half' of young people in 2011. For one thing, the term 'non-college-bound' has essentially disappeared from our vocabulary. Over the past 20 years, there has been growing public agreement that all young people need to be prepared for FE as well as careers. When high school students are asked today what they are going to do after high school, over 90 per cent say they are going on to college or university. More importantly, over 70 per cent of high school graduates do in fact go on to enrol in a HE institution. But when we ask what proportion of young Americans have earned a college or university degree by their mid-twenties, the answer is less encouraging: only 30 per cent have graduated from a four-year institution and another 10 per cent from a two-year college. If we add in another 10 per cent who have acquired a recognized one-year occupational certificate from a post-secondary education or training institution, this brings us to half the population with a meaningful post-secondary credential by age 25.

It may be an exaggeration to characterize the other half of the age cohort as 'forgotten', but in an economy in which the gap between those with post-secondary credentials and skills and those without is widening, the one-in-four young people who drop out of high school are especially vulnerable; so are those who start some form of HE but never finish. Our conclusion, looking at our high school and HE dropout data, was that if anything, the case for investing in a set of rigorous CTE pathways alongside the strictly academic pathway is even stronger today than it was 20 years ago.

This conclusion was buttressed by two sources of data. First, job projections from the Georgetown University Center on Education and the Workforce, USA, suggest that over the next decade, nearly a third of jobs will be 'middle skill' – that is, they will require some education or training beyond high school, but not necessarily a four-year degree (Carneville et al., 2010, p. 110). This projection challenges the widespread belief that the American labour market is becoming increasingly bifurcated into high-skills and low-skills occupations, and that the only good jobs in our economy will require a four-year college degree.

The second source of data we found compelling comes from two recent OECD studies, 'Learning for Jobs' (OECD, 2010a) and 'Off to a Good Start? Jobs for Youth' (OECD, 2010b). These two studies, one from the Education Directorate, the other from the Labour and Social Affairs Directorate, provide strong evidence that those European countries with the best-developed vocational education systems – especially the countries with the strongest apprenticeship programmes – manage to equip a much larger fraction of their young people with skills and credentials to make a successful transition from secondary school into the workforce, thereby significantly reducing the proportion of young people at risk of sustained unemployment at the point of entry into the labour market.

The problematic status of vocational education

When I talk with American colleagues about the virtues of the Swiss or German apprenticeship systems – that is, how these are mainstream systems, serving a broad range of students, preparing people for white-collar careers in high tech or banking as well as the traditional blue-collar trades – the first response is often: 'But don't they track students as early as age 10, something we would never condone?' Leaving aside for the moment the pervasive but subtle forms of tracking that characterize much of American education, the answer, at least for Germany, is unfortunately: 'Yes, they do track very early.' Given the history of vocational education in the United States, especially the perception that in large urban districts it has too often been a 'dumping ground' for low-income and minority youth, this is usually a conversation-stopper.

To understand this reaction, one needs to understand two things about the American system, one having to do with the twentieth-century growth and decline of vocational education; the other, with the evolution of the academic standards movement over the past two decades. The historical point is that the US vocational system, largely with the stimulus of a major piece of federal legislation in 1917, developed mostly as a separate system, organized and governed at the state level independent of academic high schools. It was not until the 1960s that there was federal support for vocational education programmes offered inside regular comprehensive high schools.

Consequently, while vocational education has taken place inside most comprehensive high schools for the last half century, its programmes have been offered on a separate track from programmes serving university-bound students. American high schools continued to function largely as sorting and selecting machines, identifying those students deemed to have the talent for higher learning and providing them with a rigorous academic education while expecting everyone else to enter the labour market directly upon graduation.

Despite our rhetoric about the democratic purposes of comprehensive high schools, by and large these institutions have been organized in ways that perpetuated existing racial and economic stratification, with low-income and minority students disproportionately concentrated in the vocational track.

With the rise of the standards movement, however, the name of the game changed. Driven largely by the dramatic changes taking place in the economy – the decline of manufacturing, the computing revolution, globalization and outsourcing of lower-skilled jobs – schools were now being asked to provide all students with a foundational level of academic skills that hitherto were expected only of the talented few. With rising academic expectations came rising accountability for results, which meant increased pressure on schools to devote more time to core academics, especially those subjects being assessed for accountability purposes, and less time for electives, including vocational education. Between 1982 and 1994 the proportion of high school students taking three or more courses in a single vocational area fell from 34 per cent to 25 per cent, and that percentage has continued to decline, especially in those states that have made the college preparatory curriculum the default curriculum for all students. While the rhetoric in today's policy environment is about all students leaving high school college-and-career ready, the reality is that almost everywhere, career readiness is on the back burner.

The new Career and Technical Education

In the past two decades new models of vocational education have emerged in the United States that demonstrate that it is possible to combine rigorous academic studies with career training in high-skill, high-demand fields. In order to differentiate these kinds of programmes from vocational education in the more traditional trades, the term 'career and technical education' (CTE) has come into use. These models are best seen in a set of national programmes that have acquired sufficient scale to become important players in the high school reform world.

Our Pathways report profiles several such programmes. Perhaps the best-known model combining strong academics with career preparation is the career academy. Career academy programmes typically enrol young people in Grade 9 (age 14) and carry them through high school graduation (age 17). There are roughly 3,000 career academies in the United States, 500 of which operate under the umbrella of the National Academy Foundation (NAF). NAF academies mainly prepare young people in four career areas – finance, engineering, ICT and hospitality and tourism – with health care set to become the fifth specialist field. A key feature of the NAF design is that all students are provided with a 6–10 week paid internship by one of 2,500 corporate partners.

NAF's engineering academies utilize curriculum developed by Project Lead the Way, a national four-year pre-engineering program now enrolling 300,000 students in 3,500 high schools across the country. Students move through a sequence of increasingly challenging courses culminating in a capstone course in engineering design and development in which they work in teams to devise a solution to an open-ended engineering problem.

High Schools That Work (HSTW) is another national network, including over 1,200 schools, mostly in the south where many high schools continue to have a strong vocational track. Unlike career academies, which are deliberately designed as a detracking strategy, the focus of HSTW has been to ensure that students in a vocational track are getting a rigorous academic education, especially in mathematics and science, albeit typically taught in a more applied fashion.

In addition to these and other national networks, many states have revamped their old vocational programmes or created new ones that combine instruction in more modern, challenging career areas with rigorous academics. One very positive consequence of the standards movement has been that it has created pressure on school districts to close down low-level, low-expectations maths and science courses that vocational students were often assigned to. In a world in which all students are required to pass assessments in maths and English based on challenging academic standards as a condition of high school graduation, there is no longer room for such courses.

One important common denominator that characterizes our strongest national and state CTE programs is that they are designed to leave open the option for successful graduates to continue on to HE, and this is in fact what most of their graduates do. Over 90 per cent of NAF graduates, for example, go on to HE, most to four-year colleges, and of these, more than half graduate in four years (by contrast, the six-year graduation rate nationally is only 56%).

A related common denominator is that these programmes typically are designed to serve a broad range of students. While African American and Latino students are often overrepresented, as are students with special needs, these programmes are not intended primarily for 'at-risk' students or students with very low academic skills. The involvement of employers in programme design and the provision of internships or other forms of work-based learning creates a set of behavioural expectations around attendance, punctuality, respectful communication, teamwork and other 'soft skills' that typically carry over into the classroom setting, creating a seriousness of purpose often missing from other high school classrooms serving similar students.

The challenge for the United States is not simply to scale up quality CTE programs like those described above, but rather to create a pathways system within which these and other effective programme models can grow and flourish. This is why the experience of the European apprenticeship countries is so relevant for countries like the United States and England. In Austria, Denmark, Finland, Germany, the Netherlands and Switzerland, one can see coherent vocational systems designed to help most young people make a successful transition from secondary school to work.

Although the design of these systems differs from country to country, there are some common elements. These systems all serve a broad range of students, between 40 and 70 per cent of the age cohort. They all offer pathways leading to qualifications in a broad range of occupations, not just the typical blue-collar trades that we associate with apprenticeships. They all combine learning at the workplace with aligned academic course work in a classroom setting. They all have substantial employer involvement in curriculum design and standard-setting in order to ensure that the qualifications graduates earn will have currency in the labour market. And all of these systems acknowledge the need to create options for graduates to continue on to further and higher education if they choose.

It is easy for American policy makers to tick off the reasons why such systems cannot (or should not) be built in the United States. These systems depend on early tracking. They expect students to make binding career choices at an early age. They require a degree of centralized planning that we would never tolerate. They are built on trade and craft traditions that we don't share. Their employers have strong incentives to participate, in part because their labour markets are more regulated than ours. Our unions would never agree to youth subminimum wages. The list goes on.

While all of these concerns have some basis in reality in one or more of these systems, they are by no means universally the case. For example, Finland and Denmark demonstrate that one can have a high-quality upper secondary vocational system without early tracking. While Germany and Switzerland ask students to choose from a bewilderingly large list of occupations, Denmark asks students to choose initially from 12 occupational clusters, and only later do students zero in on a more specific occupation. While it is true that the German labour market is highly regulated, the Swiss labour market operates much like ours and Switzerland's apprenticeship system is if anything even more impressive than Germany's. Switzerland also has one of the lowest – indeed, usually *the* lowest – rate of youth unemployment in Europe. And I don't believe any of these systems treats the apprenticeship contract as irrevocable; in fact, about 20 per cent of German apprentices switch occupations after the first year.

An American pathways system

So what would a US pathways system look like that avoided the pitfalls of tracking and drew on the best features of the strongest European systems? Given our history and culture, is it feasible to imagine that the United States could ever build a vocational education system that has at least some of the attributes of the strongest European systems? I believe the answer is yes, but it would require an approach built upon the following principles:

1   All students are provided the same common core academic curriculum at least up to Grade 10 (age 16).

2   A much-expanded investment in career information, counselling and workplace exposure beginning in the middle grades and continuing through high school.

3   All career pathways are aligned with regional labour market needs, have significant employer engagement and lead to a post-secondary credential with currency in the labour market.

4   All pathways provide continuing academic skill development – especially analytic reading, writing, communication and quantitative reasoning – integrated with CTE.

5   Enrolment in a pathway is based primarily on student and family choice, not assignment by the school.

6   All pathways are designed to leave open the possibility of FE beyond the attainment of the initial occupational certificate or degree.

These principles can best be seen in operation in Northern European countries like Finland and Denmark. While these countries do not have as well-developed apprenticeship systems as the German-speaking nations, they do have the advantage of satisfying principles 1 and 5, critically important if this approach to secondary education is ever to take root in the United States.

Finland is especially impressive in this regard. Finland has no tracking whatever up to age 16, at which point students choose between academic and vocational upper secondary schools. The fact that over 40 per cent of young Finns now opt for vocational education in a technology-driven economy suggests that it is possible to design a vocational system that can compete on a level playing field for status and resources with the university-bound system.

There are very substantial challenges that would have to be overcome in order to implement the principles enumerated above, especially number 3. Many American high schools have benefited over the years from partnership programmes with local employers. Such programmes run the gamut from modest support for sports or other extracurricular activities to scholarships for graduates to more substantial career-related initiatives involving such things as mentoring, job shadowing, work-based learning and summer internships. These latter opportunities are usually attached to career academies or other strong CTE programs with active employer advisory committees. In contrast with Northern European systems, however, US employers do not engage with our high schools with the expectation that they are helping to identify and train entry-level employees for their firm, or even the next generation of workers for their industry. Rather, the overwhelming majority of CTE programs in our schools are designed to be exploratory, to expose young people to the world of work and to motivate otherwise academically disengaged youth to understand why the acquisition of foundational literacy and quantitative reasoning skills matters in the labour market.

At bottom, a major cultural difference between US employers and those European employers who participate in apprenticeship programmes is that most US employers are deeply sceptical that 16- or 17-year-olds can add value to their firm's bottom line. This may be a chicken-and-egg phenomenon: schools don't ask employers to provide anything like European-style apprenticeship opportunities because they assume employers will refuse; employers don't offer them because they doubt that high schools could organize themselves to support such opportunities by providing the rigorous aligned academic work that could help students perform successfully in the workplace.

Organizing a pathways system: three options

Given these challenges, how might a pathways system be best organized? I see at least three major options. The first, which is already being implemented in some large urban high schools, is to universalize the career academy model. Thanks in large measure to support from the Bill and Melinda Gates Foundation and a handful of other private foundations, in cities like New York, Chicago, Boston and Philadelphia, buildings that formerly housed large dysfunctional tracked high schools with astronomically high failure rates now house several smaller schools or academies, each with a career or thematic focus. These small schools, typically serving 300–500 students, are deliberately designed to integrate academic and career preparation. They often are organized in partnership with one or more community-based organizations and almost always provide their students with internships or other forms of work or service learning opportunities. In New York City, where the small schools strategy has been mostly fully implemented, there is powerful evidence that this strategy has significantly boosted student achievement and increased high school graduation rates, especially for disadvantaged students. Even in New York, however, many of these small schools or academies have very weak or non-existent employer engagement and are focused more on high school completion than on career preparation.

In its pure form, this option would require all students to choose a career area or theme around which their high school education would be organized. Twenty years ago the state of Oregon adopted legislation based on this principle. High schools were to organize themselves into broad career majors – for example, health, environment, technology, arts and media – each designed to serve a broad range of students, and each incorporating readings, problems, examples drawn from its sector into the delivery of the core academic subjects. For a combination of reasons including funding, implementation challenges and political resistance from families focused only on university admissions, Oregon's career major programme never got fully off the ground. This suggests that attempting to weave career preparation into the secondary education experience of all children, at least in the US setting, may not be viable politically.

A middle ground option that would not require schools to take on the political challenge of tampering with the academics-only university pathway is to build a set of four-year career-focused pathways that would coexist alongside the academics-only pathway. Again, the NAF career academy provides a useful model. If all students other than those on the academics-only path could choose among a limited set of career academies (e.g. health, finance, ICT, engineering, tourism), all of which provided integrated career preparation and academics and genuinely prepared people for HE as well as employment, this would not only ameliorate the concerns of parents wanting an academics-only programme, but it would also reduce the anxieties of those who fear a return to tracking.

This is the strategy being pursued by an ambitious California programme called Linked Learning. With funding from the James Irvine

Foundation, Linked Learning is developing career academies in such major California industry sectors as building and environmental design, biomedical and health sciences and arts, media and entertainment. Each academy is designed in such a way as to meet the academic course-taking requirements for admission to California's four-year universities as well as providing advanced technical preparation in a career area.

The third option would be to follow the example of Northern Europe and move towards a system in which there is a sharper distinction between lower and upper secondary education. This would defer the choice of a career area until Grade 11 (age 16), enabling schools to concentrate on ensuring that all students acquire a solid foundation of academic knowledge and skills, especially in reading, writing and mathematics. This would not preclude schools from using career interests and themes and applied learning strategies to deliver core academics in the lower secondary grades, but it would allow for two more years of full-time academics.

In order for the United States to develop a version of vocational upper secondary education at all comparable to the strongest European systems, we would have to link the last two years of high school with an additional year or two of post-secondary education or training, typically at a community college. This approach, while creating the significant logistical and funding challenges associated with programmes that cross institutional boundaries, has one major advantage: US employers are much more likely to be willing to participate in occupational certificate or degree programmes organized by post-secondary institutions than by high schools. In this option one would begin by establishing an agreement between the post-secondary provider and an employer group mapping backward from the certificate requirements in a particular field and then build a three- or four-year pathway starting in Grade 11 (age 16) that would include paid internships and summer employment opportunities while in high school with the appropriate sequence of academic and technical courses leading to a certificate or degree.

Programmes that span secondary and post-secondary education are increasingly popular with families in the United States, partly because the costs of HE continue to rise. Thanks largely to the Gates Foundation, we now have a national network of 230 Early College High

Schools (ECHS), serving approximately 50,000 students, mostly low-income and minority. These schools all have formal relationships with a two- or four-year college or university. The idea behind early college is to accelerate the learning of these students by placing them in college-level courses so that by the time they graduate high school they have already accumulated at least one year of college credits. Nearly one-quarter of ECHS students are now graduating with a two-year associate's degree, and over 40 per cent with at least one year of college credit. Although most of these schools are not explicitly career-focused, in many instances the college courses students take are in career and technical fields, and there is considerable interest within the ECHS network in creating more formal CTE pathways leading to occupational certification or a technical two-year degree.

Implications of the US experience for England

I have been asked to comment on the debate about the organizational structure of schooling, specifically about the merits of moving from an age 11–16 system to a secondary education structure that serves 14–18-year-olds. For better or worse, this has been a settled issue in the United States for generations. We continue to debate about whether the middle grades should be connected to elementary schools or should be in separate middle schools (typically Grades 6–8 – ages 11–14), but our high schools overwhelmingly serve 14–17-year-olds, and for all our complaints about the quality of high school education, virtually no one argues that younger students should be incorporated into these schools.

As you might infer from my description above of the third pathways option, I think the prospect of adding 18-year-olds gives England an important opportunity to differentiate the lower and upper secondary years and build a two- or three-year youth apprenticeship model into the upper grades. Given the concerns raised in the Wolf Report about the number of students entering vocational education with problematic English and maths skills (Wolf, 2011), and given the weak labour market returns for those pursuing low-level vocational qualifications, there is an argument for concentrating significant attention in the first two years of secondary education to shoring up weak academic skills before sending students out for work-based learning.

For both of our countries, though, I would advocate a pragmatic, build-on-what-works strategy in the near term. Despite my own personal preference for the third option, I strongly support the idea of expanding career academies or other programmes that are effectively serving students from the beginning of the lower secondary years, especially if they are engaging students who might otherwise fall by the wayside. The UTCs just getting underway in England seem an especially promising model for combining academic and career preparation, with the balance between the two goals shifting in the upper grades to more focus on the career side. University sponsorship sends a powerful signal that strong career preparation programmes can and should be designed to leave the door open to HE, a central message we have tried to send in our Pathways report.

If the core premise underlying the old tracking system was that some young people needed to be prepared for college and others for careers, the core premise of the pathways approach is that all young people need to be prepared both for careers and further learning. Further learning need not necessarily take place in a HE institution, but all young people will need the foundational skills and intellectual dispositions to acquire new knowledge and adapt to changing circumstances over a working lifetime. A narrow, occupationally focused education is unlikely to equip young people with those skills, which is why it is critical to ensure that all students leave school with a solid academic foundation.

I want to close by returning to the lessons for both of our countries that England's northern European neighbours can provide. For all of their differences, countries like Switzerland, Germany, the Netherlands, Denmark and Finland teach us that it is possible to build secondary education systems on the premise that all young people need to be educated for a vocation or calling, that all vocations are worthy of serious preparation and that the best preparation comes out of a well-organized, well-defined partnership among educators, employers and employee associations. While some vocations require university preparation, most don't; but all require a mix of classroom-based and workplace-based learning. Unless and until we are prepared to invest in building rigorous, robust pathways across the occupational spectrum that can prepare all young people for a life of satisfying work and further learning, and to give young people the academic support and information needed to make appropriate choices among pathways, we will never overcome the legacy of a two-tiered, heavily tracked education system that predictably replicates social and economic inequality from one generation to the next.

7

STRUCTURE AND THE INDIVIDUAL: AN INDEPENDENT SCHOOL PERSPECTIVE

Andrew Halls

Picture 7.1 King's College School, Wimbledon.

I have been a teacher within the independent sector for 31 years, 14 of them as a headmaster – first at Magdalen College School, Oxford, and now at King's College School in Wimbledon. As a boy, I was educated in the state system, and attended a large, then new, comprehensive school in Birmingham for the whole of my secondary education. I have often been aware of how much we who now teach in the independent sector have learned either from our time within maintained schools, or through observation of them and the good practice they represent. But I can also see that the independent sector, often criticized for elitism or for calculated antiquarianism, has sometimes set the standards, and offered answers, too. When it comes to ages of transfer, the independent sector has some solutions of its own, but has also proved skilful in adapting the best of maintained school practice. Most of all, however, it has generally been uncompromising in recognizing that different types of learners need different types of teaching, and different opportunities in order to thrive. In this way, its practice makes explicit what is implicit in the proposal contained within this book: vocational and academic education are of identical importance, but depend on completely different means of delivery.

The 'great public school tradition' assumes a transfer not at 11, nor at 14, but at 13. Historically, this is when boys, and it was almost invariably boys, would begin their time at what were and in some cases remain, the most famous schools in the world. Eton, Harrow and many other boarding schools all followed this model, and it remains common among top independent schools to this day, including such leading London day schools as King's College School, Westminster and St Paul's. However, it is rare for girls to transfer at 13. The influence of the Girls' Day Schools' Trust whose schools were essentially fee-charging grammar schools (grammar schools invariably recruiting at 11) and the fact that far fewer girls were traditionally sent away from home to board have together meant there is a powerful tradition of girls in the independent sector transferring at 11. Preparatory schools, jealously guarding their boys in senior year groups and ever-anxious that the great boys' schools will move to an 11+ entry, have long accepted that they cannot keep bright girls after Year 6.

There are several reasons for many independent schools preferring the transfer of boys at the age of 13, not all equally convincing. First of all, there is the slightly absurd but nevertheless potent one: 'We have always done it this way.' History, particularly within boys' boarding schools, is a powerful master. The sometimes feral nature of dormitory life meant that it was easier and more humane if the boys who left the comparative gentleness of their families or prep schools had at least begun to embark on the journey to adulthood – that is, hit puberty – before their arrival. Once at the senior school, they would find themselves immersed in the extraordinary and sometimes unsettlingly unaccountable microcosm of their boarding house. As the iconoclastic film 'If' showed all too sharply, a weak housemaster depended on favoured senior boys to keep order, and although the film has never been accused of subtlety, even those of us who began our teaching in the 1980s could still recognize aspects of this corrupt and corrupting world, albeit by then limited mainly to the worst and worst-led boarding schools.

Still, this cannot alone explain the survival of the 13+ entry point to so many leading schools. There is also the relationship that exists between the leading 13+ entry schools, and their 'feeder' schools – the thousands of preparatory schools which exist to guide pupils into the most appropriate senior schools. Such schools are unapologetic in providing their pupils with a wide range of traditional subjects, invariably including all three sciences, Latin and often Greek, and these are duly tested in the common entrance papers, or, even more fearsome, scholarship papers, when the children are 13 and ready to transfer to their senior school. Schools such as mine are well aware of how much excellent understanding of the basics is achieved through the teaching, often highly traditional, but also sometimes inspirational, at the prep schools. Indeed, the best prep schools sometimes suspect that it is their teaching, not that provided by the senior school, that has really laid the foundations for a pupil's later success in life.

When I became Master of Magdalen College School, Oxford, in 1998, the school was languishing in the league tables and had a diminishing reputation locally as tired and complacent. This was not entirely fair, but the impression was widespread. I can remember being told in my first year more than once by shrewd Oxford dons who were former parents of the school that their sons had won their place to Cambridge or Oxford thanks to all that they had been taught at north Oxford's famous prep school, The Dragon, before they even got to Magdalen College School. The point was double-edged: the prep school education had been outstanding, but that provided by the school I had inherited was too often lacklustre. This soon became an accusation that was never levelled again, as MCS moved inexorably towards the top of all league tables, and more and more boys won places at the best universities as a result of their MCS education. However, it reflects on the power and the capacity of great prep schools to affect so much in their pupils' development. This being so, many strong independent schools naturally are happy to remain with the 13+ entry, knowing that their pupils will indeed be 'prepared': well taught in all important subjects, used to clear-cut codes of discipline and encouraged at an early age to develop the 'whole man' through sport, drama, music and clubs.

For weaker boarding schools, the prep schools offer something of a lifeline, too. Parents of boys who are unable to win places at the strong independent day schools in their local area are often unwilling to countenance the next level of day school down the list: they may after all have names the parent has 'never heard of' – or worse, their friends have never heard of. Regardless of its merits, such a school will find itself overlooked as parents seek to repair their battered pride by sending their son to a historic boarding school. They know that its standard of entry is low, but a lustre still attaches itself to its name, and the prep school can assure them that an all-rounder scholarship will ease the fee burden, while incidentally adding a valuable new entry to their own honours boards.

But if some of this sounds, and indeed is, cynical, it is important to remember that there are sound educational and developmental reasons for the 13+ transition, too. A child is able to achieve much at his prep school, surrounded by younger children, and this can include prefecture and positions of responsibility in Years 7 and 8. Parents of fast-developing 11- and 12-year-olds also take comfort in the belief that they have kept at bay some of the unwanted influences they fear exist within schools where innocent 11-year-olds are taught next to a classroom of wild 16-year-olds. An exaggerated fear, perhaps, but not an uncommon one.

Pupils at such prep schools receive a formal but broad and stimulating education, and then transfer at the beginning of Year 9, aged 13, to a senior school. The senior school then has one year in which to offer an extremely wide choice of subjects so that boys, and their teachers, begin to see where their main talents lie. This first year of senior school is always one of the hardest to timetable precisely because good schools want every pupil to experience as many subjects, sports and activities as possible. The 13+ transfer also means that children have a year to settle in without feeling the pressure of public examinations, whose courses begin in earnest in Year 10.

At my current school, we are lucky enough to have an outstanding junior school, and this, too, teaches boys through to the age of 13 rather than 11. In other words, when the prep school boys join the senior school at 13, so do the King's junior boys, and all are mixed together in new forms and sets. However, as I suggested at the beginning, we may have something to learn from the comprehensive I attended as a boy.

Shenley Court School, Birmingham, was a purpose-built comprehensive, and when I went there in 1970, it was still very new, and full of optimism. Facilities to my young eyes, used to the cramped domesticities of late 1960s primary and infant schools, seemed extraordinary. It had at least two school halls, spacious grounds and, most miraculously of all, a swimming pool. More dauntingly, it was also a school of 1,800 boys and girls aged 11–18 from every sort of background imaginable. I was taught alongside the children of writers and academics, and those whose fathers were serving prisoners. To accommodate such diversity, the school, in those days, not only streamed us quite rigorously, but divided us into three sections – a lower, middle and an upper school. Each section or 'school' had not only its own building, from which we strayed only to attend science or games lessons in specialized and shared accommodation, but even its own playground. One of the very few rules any of us tended to obey without question was that on no account was anyone ever allowed onto the wrong playground.

Sadly, Shenley Court, like so many other glistening new-build comprehensives, fell into both physical and educational decay; in subsequent years it frequently seemed to be in special measures. Recently, I heard it was to be demolished: the new buildings which had so impressed me 40 years ago had aged with terrible speed and inevitability. However, I can see that, in some ways, my old comprehensive was ahead of the game. Even if its ruthless division into sections had its root in the fact that the school was too big, there was educational good sense in the school's structure. Optimistic and rather naïve 11-year-olds were taught under one roof, and felt protected.

Since those days, many schools in both the maintained and independent sectors have reproduced the structure, although some schools in the independent sector were slow to adopt the model which they associated with a state sector for which they felt hidden disdain. My previous school was one which had tried to run its pastoral and academic systems on a purely house basis, slicing the pupils into six vertical house segments. Such a system certainly had its advantages – at least potentially. However, in reality, it was misplaced in a day school, especially one which took most of its boys at the age of 11. Younger boys needed more structure than a sometimes laissez faire house system modelled on that which prevailed at boarding schools. In an academic day school one of the obvious dangers was that not every one of the six heads of house could be equally expert in every aspect of university admissions, to take just one glaring example. Nor might they all share the same disciplinary expectations, to take a second. The easy-going tolerance with which an idle or weak housemaster indulges a sixth former may or may not do lasting harm, but applied to 11-year-olds the damage will be certain.

For these, and other reasons, I introduced section heads to represent the lower school (Years 7 and 8 with students aged between 11 and 13), the middle school (9–11 with students aged between 13 and 16) and the sixth form (with students aged between 16 and 18). The house system survived, and, I think, was strengthened, not least because pupils enjoyed much more support. Year group issues, such as the not inconsiderable one of public exams in Years 11 and 13, could be foreseen and addressed by staff whose responsibility it was to consider the needs of a year group, rather than a tutor acting alone with his or her little vertical slice of the school, often feeling directionless or even isolated. The sections worked well, although it would have been just as possible for the lower school to include Year 9, and I often wondered whether this would be better.

At King's, the Junior School headmaster has appointed a head of Years 7 and 8, while in the senior school, I have created a head of middle school (Years 9–11) and strengthened the role of head of sixth form. None of these moves weaken what at King's was already an exceptionally strong and supportive house system, but the symbolism of a pastoral system which operates both vertically and horizontally is powerful, and the effect highly supportive of every pupil.

The majority of independent schools with pupils aged 11–18 on the same premises have divided their school into what is effectively a lower, a middle and an upper school, and they have done so for educational, pastoral, behavioural and organizational reasons. Sometimes the division is in name only, and pupils from Year 7 spend much of their time in the company of older pupils, but in the best examples, lower school boys and girls will have a sense of a physical separateness for recreation, and, in many cases, teaching spaces.

A well-organized lower school model means that children new to a senior school, and still physically and emotionally quite immature, have a champion who is relatively senior within the school structure – the head of lower school – and can feel that their concerns are taken account of in an appropriate way. Their section head will ensure the homework burden is not too excessive, and see that simple but important issues, such as playing areas, lunch sittings, petty or hurtful behaviour by word, text or deed, or something as basic as the availability of drinking fountains, are actively addressed. Similarly, a head of middle school eases pupils through their first ever public exams, and the difficulties of choosing A-level subjects. A good head of sixth form has a miraculous rapport with 16–18-year-olds, able to keep good discipline without causing alienation, setting standards, without allowing often highly sophisticated and ambitious young men and women to feel patronized or unnecessarily chivvied. Each section thus has its own requirements – not just in terms of timetabling or location, but in the very character of the men and women placed in their charge.

And this is why I think the proposal at the heart of this book makes such sense for the education of boys and girls throughout this country, and not only those at independent schools like mine. A break, and one which contains within it an assessment, whether at 13 or 14, enables schools to have a much clearer idea as to the aptitudes of the boys and girls in their charge, and the paths they might wish to take through their lives. The old grammar school watershed at 11+ worked for many but by no means all: even as it was, boys had to be allowed a lower passmark than girls in their 11+ exams because they were more immature. By 14, these concerns can hardly be levelled at a system which is trying earnestly to match the education it offers to the character of each child in its care.

The proposal enables us at last to face an essential truth about humanity that apologists for comprehensive schools have set their faces against for far too long: that people are different, and children vary as much as adults, perhaps more so, in the needs and expectations they each have – academically, in skills and in expectations. The 16-year-old boy who does not want to study poetry by Carol Ann Duffy is not necessarily a philistine; he might actually have an understanding of what he likes, and what he wants to contribute to the world. It just may not be within a traditional academic, or too often, pseudo-academic, curriculum.

Although many independent school heads speak warmly about the catholicity of intake that characterizes their schools, the reality is that most either apply rigorous academic selection, or wish they could do so but operate in a market where this is not possible. Why should it be that where schools have freedom they exert it by selecting on academic principles, when the whole mind-set of modern educational philosophy is predisposed in favour of non-academic entry procedures? Even Margaret Thatcher allowed most of the remaining grammar schools in the early 1980s to be transformed into comprehensive schools, and no government for 40 years or more has spoken up for academic selection.

I often talk to an ex-grammar school headmaster who is now in his mid-eighties. His school was in a socially diverse and challenging urban area in the Midlands. Even now, he still hears from pupils who tell him that their opportunity to learn alongside other similarly disposed children in a grammar school transformed their lives. In 1974, it was decreed that his school could no longer select by ability. He recalls ruefully that whereas pleas to the local authority to mend broken heating systems or windows went unanswered for months, the day the decision to turn his school into a comprehensive was made, a council worker in overalls arrived promptly at the school gates – to paint out the word 'grammar' from the school sign.

With the demise of state-provided selective education, whereby bright boys and girls from the bleakest and most challenging of homes could attend a school like the one referred to above, and become, like so many in the 1950s, 1960s and 1970s, the first of their family to attend university, social mobility in the United Kingdom spluttered to a halt. Many surveys have shown that such upward mobility virtually ceased in the United Kingdom in the mid-1970s, just as the comprehensive system became all-prevailing. Modern grammar schools, in leafy suburbs and colonized by the middle class, serve no such function – only 2 per cent of their pupils are on free school meals. Many independent schools will have a more diverse social range than this.

It is not only history that shows the success of allowing children of similar ability to be taught together, nor the example of privileged independent schools. In those areas where grammar schools still exist, the competition for places is terrifying. We can safely assume this would not be the case if grammar schools were not seen to be highly successful. A free market, in other words, recognizes all too clearly what no major political party is prepared to admit: academic selection not only works, it is popular. Some grammar school heads have admitted that to pass their 11+ examinations, boys and girls need to score almost perfect marks, such are the numbers competing to secure the educational equivalent of a winning lottery ticket. There is no shortage of customers for a place at a school where staff are able to set high standards – and the reason they can set these standards is simple: it is because children at their school are united in a common aim, and able to respond to a particular teaching style and curriculum.

We can see, then, that the desire for education suited to the character of the child exists. We can see that in the past it worked much better than our current one-size-fits-all educational economy. We can see that children with a vocational leaning are not well supported in our schools, for all the loud claims of the comprehensive partisans. But we also know that we are not allowed to say this, let alone do anything about it.

There is, in fact, reason within the madness of this hypocrisy. The old grammar school system worked well for the few, but not the many. Time has shown us that the comprehensive system works badly for just about everyone, but, understandably, no one would wish to replace it with a nakedly elitist throw-back that was even in its own time neither fair nor equitable. One of the great failings of the educational system that allowed grammar schools such privilege and influence was that too little care was taken of those who did not pass the 11+ examination.

Whereas the intention behind the Education Act of 1944 had been to look after all types of children with equal care, the technology colleges proposed within the Act were rarely built, too few grammar schools were opened, and the secondary modern schools were often associated with failure. For these reasons, the move to comprehensive schooling was well-intentioned and compassionate, as indeed was the school I attended as a boy. It was not the fault of the school, or its teachers, that even during my seven years there it began to trace a downward path which seems hardly ever to have been arrested in the decades since. The same happened to countless other schools, and the fall was saddest and cruellest in the once-great grammar schools, previously beacons in their locals areas, pulled down into the all-engulfing sludge of well-meant mediocrity.

However, a tiered structure could retain the best of both systems. It would allow pupils to be taught together in what we might call a lower school during that crucial period of development and self-discovery between the ages of 11 and 14. Then, quite distinct pathways would open up before them. The pressure for 10-year-olds to pass selective exams would not exist, and teachers would have longer to assess each child to see which way their talents might take them. There is no need to return to the creation of stand-alone middle schools, an experiment that had petered out almost completely by the start of this century, because the lower school 'section' within a main school, as outlined above, can offer similar levels of security and preparation for the next phase of a child's education.

However, this is where it is crucial to recognize that structures, however well-designed, are not sufficient in themselves. Under this system, every child, during their lower school years, would need to be assured, absolutely guaranteed, of personal and unhurried attention from appropriate staff to his or her future options. Simply creating the school tiers will not guarantee success: it will be the human engagement, the personal support of each child, that will make the changes successful. Time spent with the child and, where possible, the parents, by the tutor or advisor, would be invaluable.

This sort of personal attention is an area where the independent sector has much experience and good practice to share. I am full of admiration for the way colleagues at most independent schools give up countless unpaid hours to support the children in their care. Extra lessons for examination groups, holiday trips, Saturday sports, drama, music, innumerable pastoral meetings with pupils, parents or guardians whether advising on behaviour or motivation or helping with a family difficulty, catch-up lessons or subject 'clinics' in lunch hours all mean that pupils and staff in such schools enjoy a relationship of mutual trust. This enables colleagues to help their tutees or form members with subject choices, UCAS statements and university selection, just as they could help, were this needed, with post-14 pathway choices.

In such a system, each child would undertake a four-year course of study in which they focused on areas where they had most chance of success. For some, this course would be an academic one. It would be likely to include nine or ten GCSEs and three or four A-levels, and prepare the pupils for a university education. For others, the last phase of school life would include the study of literacy and numeracy, but practical and vocational skills would be the main focus.

The schools, or the school areas, in which vocational education would occur would not be second-best. Indeed, they may require greater funding. Certainly, they would need to establish the highest standards because their mission would be of incalculable importance. It would be to achieve a belief in the value of trade, skills, entrepreneurialism or self-betterment for the non-academic that we have not seen in the United Kingdom since Edwardian times. In other words, this programme would have nothing to do with passing or failing – and everything to do with matching children's talents or abilities to the right course or pathway.

I mentioned 'school areas' in the paragraph above, because it would be perfectly possible for some schools to combine the different pathways – academic, entrepreneurial and vocational – on the same site where this was appropriate to the size and capacity of the school. What would be essential would be for schools to stop feeling embarrassed about those boys and girls who prefer vocational courses, and instead to feel immense pride and excitement in their talents, harnessing them so that they learn to make something of the individual they actually are.

We know that employers are often unimpressed with the work ethos and skills of British youth; often, they feel they have learned precious little in their 11 years of compulsory education. They feel no confidence that their staying on for another 2 years will change very much. If we can adapt our education system to respond to the differentness of our children, and move away from the well-meaning but destructive homogeneity of discredited twentieth-century educational squeamishness, we will have done the future generations of this once powerful and creative country an enormous favour. As David Harbourne points out elsewhere in this book, some other countries look after their young people much better than we do. He notes that in Austria, where there is both pride and purpose in vocational training, 80 per cent of young people select a vocational route after 14, Austrian unemployment was running at 4.2 per cent in July 2011, and on average it takes less than 6 months to find a job after leaving education in Austria as compared to nearly 17 months in 12 other European countries.

Taking the best practice from the past, the present and from both home and abroad, we should have the faith and courage to jettison all that stands between a child and his or her potential – all the bad practice, all the prejudice, all the specious pseudo-academic flimflam and all the wrong-headed timidity. In their place, and by means of scrupulous advice and guidance within new structures that reflect and celebrate the different aptitudes and ambitions of each child in our care, we can build a school system that actually works. That may not be good news for independent schools, not a few of which owe their survival to the perceived failure of local maintained schools – but it will be good news for the 92 per cent of children whose education is overseen by the state. And it will be electrifying for the prospects of this country in a century that looks set to test inherited Western complacency to breaking-point.

8

EDUCATION ON A HUMAN SCALE: A MIDDLE SCHOOL PERSPECTIVE

David Brandon-Bravo

Leaving a small primary school at the age of 11 to start in a huge comprehensive school was an experience which took me years to recover from. It was not just the comparative size of the school buildings, although they were daunting enough, nor the intimidation of significantly larger pupils who were frequently loud, rude and often frighteningly aggressive. Most of all it was the complete culture change which had the longest lasting negative impact. In my last year of primary school I had been one of a class of thirty 11-year-olds who made up half the year group. We had a single class teacher, Mr Coles, whom we all adored. I was an individual who was known by everyone – teachers, pupils and support staff alike. I was a creative, imaginative, happy and secure boy. That is what 11-year-olds should be – children, not early-onset adolescents. In the shadow of the secondary school I disappeared.

Ralph, a close friend of mine, recently arrived for a visit from California and was reintroduced to my children whom he had not seen for several years. My son had just started secondary school and Ralph engaged him in conversation about the school, chatting with him about what he liked and disliked. Then came Ralph's moment of disbelief. 'Are you seriously telling me', he said, 'that little Alexander is in a school of 1,200 students through to the age of 18! Seriously? Does he mix at break and lunchtime with 15 and 16-year-olds, does he try to compete with them in the soccer yard, brave the toilets, get to the front of a queue for food?'

Ralph was incredulous; why would a country do this to its children? For Ralph our system seemed ridiculous; the needs of the junior high school kid (in American terminology) are so different from the needs of the high school student. What would putting them all together hope to achieve?

As a secondary-trained history teacher it had never occurred to me to teach in any phase of education other than secondary. To be honest, apart from primary and secondary I was not aware that any other phases in schooling existed. However, my first appointment as a newly qualified teacher was at a Milton Keynes secondary school where the youngest pupils in the school were 12 (Year 8) when they started. This was obviously different to my own experience where the age of transfer was 11, in line with most of the rest of the country. Why Buckinghamshire had a later transfer age was unclear to me at the time.

With the introduction of the National Curriculum in the 1980s, concerns soon began to be voiced that the completion of the new Key Stage 2 at the end of Year 6 (age 11) would make it difficult for the middle schools to know what to do with the Year 7 pupils prior to starting at secondary school. These concerns focused on the issues of transition and splitting schemes of work in the middle of a Key Stage; Year 7 was in danger of becoming a wasted year. Curiously, most of us felt that the Year 8 pupils were quite young enough to be starting at secondary school without making them start any earlier. Nevertheless, Milton Keynes altered the age of transfer to align it with the end of Key Stage 2 and at the same time, changed middle schools into primary schools.

The question lingered as to why the Key Stages had been carved up in the fashion that they had. On the face of it, Key Stage 2 ended in Year 6 when children are aged 11 because that was when primary education ended. But *why* was primary education concluded in Year 6? Answer: because the Factory Acts of the nineteenth century had brought state-funded education to an end at that age so that children could work down the mines, in the fields or indeed in the factories as soon as the parliamentary do-gooders would allow them to, without causing a monstrous humanitarian outcry.

The National Curriculum Key Stages that were introduced in the 1980s served to reinforce the status quo and international comparisons to identify natural points of transfer from one educational establishment to another were never seriously considered, let alone theories of child development developed by Piaget and others.

My secondary education began at a time when the compulsory minimum school leaving age was changing from 15 to 16. All over the country additional buildings were being built to accommodate the ROSLA (Raising of School Leaving Age) pupils. In South Croydon, where I grew up, it also coincided with the introduction of comprehensive schools. However, not every school in South Croydon became a comprehensive. The secondary moderns became comprehensives but the selective grammars remained selective grammars and the private fee-paying schools remained with the curious misnomer, public schools. The egalitarian leanings of my father to have me educated in a comprehensive school stumbled at the first hurdle because many parents chose not to play by the same rules: they bought into a selective or fee-paying system for their children.

In theory, my huge comprehensive should have been able to cater for all abilities. In practice, many of its teachers lacked any experience of teaching O-level syllabuses; indeed, many had never taught pupils capable of taking O-levels. We stumbled our way through to 16 when those that could, made a break for the grammar schools and those that could not went to work for the post office. I floundered somewhere in between.

Unbeknown to me at the time, many local education authorities were introducing middle schools as an alternative to comprehensive schools; they were introducing the three-tier system. In Bedfordshire, for example, the age of transfer had been thought through and it was considered appropriate for children to move from lower schools to middle schools at the age of 9, then to upper schools at 13. Across the country there were variations on this theme.

Middle schools offered a transition between little and large. From the age of 9, children had access to specialist facilities, such technology workshops, science labs, cookery rooms, and to specialist subject teachers. At a time when a broad and balanced curriculum was considered essential, middle schools proved to be very successful. Large upper schools worked with two or three feeder middle schools and the process of selecting subjects to take at O-level or CSE began at a time when pupils had been given access to a wide range of educational opportunities which enabled their choices to be informed.

Having completed an MBA (Master of Business Administration) at the University of Leicester I was looking for my next career move and applied to a Leicestershire school. When submitting my application it never crossed my mind that it was anything other than a secondary school of the kind I was accustomed to. Being shown around the school by an enthusiastic deputy head, however, I soon became aware that there were no older pupils in this school. The atmosphere was exciting, dynamic even, but the age range was from 10 to 14. This was not what I had expected, but I was so impressed by the staff and the pupils that I accepted the position of head of faculty.

I was soon converted to a system which valued and nurtured children in their middle years and specialized in their needs. I subsequently was appointed as a deputy head in a Hertfordshire middle school, followed by the headship of Parkfields Middle School in Toddington, Bedfordshire. I have just completed my eleventh year as head.

On average, we have 480 pupils aged between 9 and 13. There are 4 main feeder lower schools, but take pupils from no fewer than 18 in total: this is a reflection of the enduring popularity of the school and the widely held recognition that at Parkfields, children flourish, learn and grow – which is indeed our motto. We have recently taken over the county provision for deaf children and believe passionately in caring for vulnerable children.

We foster excellent relationships with feeder lower schools, ensuring transition is as seamless as possible. Children coming from these schools are excited but understandably anxious and the process of transition is handled with extreme sensitivity. The younger children are eased into a secondary-style education within their own teaching block, and are taught by primary-trained teachers. As soon as children start at the school they have access to the specialist facilities of science studios, technology workshops, cookery and textile rooms, ICT, art and music suites.

Subject leaders are specialists in their subjects and ensure continuity across the age range and in their liaison with lower and upper school colleagues. While literacy is the key cross-curricular skill, the curriculum nevertheless remains broad and balanced with all children studying the full range of academic subjects. Sport is a significant feature of the success of the school embodying for each pupil the ethos of personal self-improvement within a supportive team environment. Not surprisingly, the school does exceptionally well in sporting events, even when competing against much larger schools.

We have supported and continue to support other schools facing difficulties in the local area, both in leadership and teaching. We regard everything we do to be of benefit to the whole community and this is celebrated each year in a conference which Parkfields hosts for all Bedfordshire middle schools. In turn, the school is held in high esteem: in July 2012, for example, Ofsted inspected the school and judged it outstanding, saying that 'pupils flourish in an environment that fosters their academic progress and broader social development exceptionally well.'.

Pupils complete their accelerated Key Stage 3 in Year 8 by condensing a three-year course into two. This puts them a year ahead of the national average. They move to the upper school in Year 9 (age 13) able to embrace a wide set of options.

Year 8 is the great finale for pupils at Parkfields. With their final assessment complete the whole year works on a final production with casts as large as 70, while other pupils in the year group work on set design, costumes, make-up and marketing. Seeing Year 8 pupils act, sing and dance in such productions as Annie, Guys and Dolls and Bugsy Malone is testament to the levels of confidence these pupils have.

The final leavers' assembly celebrates the oldest pupils' achievements over the previous four years. The younger pupils are inspired each year by both this and the production recognizing that it is just a matter of time before it is their turn.

This brings me to the question which should always be asked: what is the role of a school? Are we simply preparing children for exams which at any given point of time are considered to be the yardstick for success or failure? Is a school's purpose to act as a sieve which selects those who will go on to pursue A-levels and then a university education and reject the rest? Or should we – as I firmly believe – hold out for a wider sense of purpose?

In many primary schools, class teachers focus relentlessly on the requirements of literacy and numeracy SATs at both Key Stages 1 and 2 (age 5–11). Teachers in many secondary schools take a similarly narrow view, believing that preparation for exams begins as soon as the children walk through their doors. Enough molly coddling, now it is time to get on with what really matters – preparation for GCSEs! One does not have to scratch very far below the surface to realize that the raison d'être for everything that goes on in secondary education is to maximize the percentage of students gaining at least five A–C passes (including maths and English) at GCSE or their equivalent. And as for those that don't . . .?

Prior to studying for a Post Graduate Certificate in Education (PGCE) I taught history at the Italia Conti stage school. The 18 months I worked there sowed seeds which have guided me through my career and have been an inspiration to my headship. The pupils were not necessarily the most academically able pupils I would teach but they were the most exciting young people I have ever met. Each of them had their talent in the performance arts recognized and this gave them the self-confidence to have a go at anything that came their way.

In recent years I have been in contact with many former Italia Conti pupils and have been delighted to hear of their successes in whatever they subsequently went on to do. Many have sought careers in the entertainment industry but others have found success in education, commerce or business.

I learned from this early teaching experience the fundamental educational concept that every child has to have the opportunity to be good at something and to be recognized for that talent, so as to enable them to succeed in whatever they subsequently choose to do. It is the moral imperative that should guide us all. In order for this to be achieved, schools have to be prepared to offer as wide an opportunity to explore what each child is good at and then to celebrate their achievement. This, rather than preparation for GCSEs and A-levels, should surely be the guiding principle for all schools.

Middle schools offer the opportunity for children aged between 9 and 13 to flourish and grow in a comparatively small and secure environment before making the choices which will affect the rest of their lives. By the age of 13, children are far more aware of where their strengths lie and the opportunities to develop these should be taken full advantage of. Middle schools offer the chance for children to experience a broad and balanced curriculum in a climate free from the crushing oppression of GCSEs. They nurture children and give them time to enjoy both education and their childhood because they recognize that the middle years are – and should be – a period of tremendous change and development. This should be celebrated and supported, not ignored and neglected.

9

LEARNING FROM OTHERS

David Harbourne

Educationalists, journalists and politicians have increasingly questioned whether GCSE grades are a reliable guide to the success of individual young people, their schools or English education as a whole. It is claimed that standards have fallen over the years because of changes to the curriculum, modular courses, questionable assessment methods, competition between awarding organizations and the effects of performance tables, which are said to encourage schools to steer pupils towards 'easier' exams in 'easier' subjects.

As Mike Tomlinson argues in Chapter 4, every major comparator country has recorded sharp increases in the number of students passing their school leaving examinations over the past four decades. Nevertheless, some countries appear – on some measures, at least – to have done better than we have here in England.

Against this background, there has been a growing interest in international tests which measure young people's skills at a given age. The Secretary of State for Education, Michael Gove, frequently quotes countries and provinces ('jurisdictions') whose students perform well in the OECD's Programme for International Student Assessment (PISA), which assesses the reading, maths and science skills of young people at the age of about 14.

PISA tests taken by young people in 2009 resulted in England being ranked twenty-seventh out of 65 countries for mathematics, twenty-fifth for reading and sixteenth for science. When the results were announced, Mr Gove said: 'Today's PISA report underlines the urgent need to reform our school system. We need to learn from the best-performing countries' and went on to compare England with high-performing jurisdictions such as Alberta (Canada), Singapore, Finland, Hong Kong and South Korea (Department for Education Press Release, 7 December 2010).

This interest in international comparisons was reflected in the remit of the review of the National Curriculum in England, launched in 2011. The review's objectives included:

- ensuring that the content of our National Curriculum compares favourably with the most successful international curricula in the highest performing jurisdictions, reflecting the best collective wisdom we have about how children learn and what they should know; and

- setting rigorous requirements for pupil attainment, which measure up to those in the highest performing jurisdictions in the world. (Department for Education, 2011e)

No one would deny the value of learning from others. However, there are significant risks in focusing on PISA alone – a point made by Tim Oates, chosen by the secretary of state to chair the expert panel on the review of the National Curriculum:

Highlighting the importance of using evidence from international comparisons is not arguing for naïve descent into policy borrowing – '. . . country X has been successful in PISA so therefore we need to do exactly what they are doing . . .'. For example, there may be a temptation to say '. . . Finland is regarded by all as superlative . . . let's see how they teach.' (2010, p. 10)

Oates drew on an analysis of Finnish maths teaching carried out by Paul Andrews in 2010. Andrews noted – among other things – that success depends on a number of factors, including an expectation of high levels of parental involvement in learning. His conclusion, as recorded by Tim Oates, is that 'simply to import Finnish classroom practice into the UK would be a gross error' (2010, p. 10).

He is quite right, of course. The list of countries which perform well in PISA tests includes some – Korea and Singapore, for example – which are socially, politically and economically very different from England. Any number of factors may have a bearing on the performance of their education systems. Parental attitudes are especially important. So, too, is the progress – or lack of it – which children make in their early years. Then there is the recruitment, initial training and continuing professional development of teachers. In short, we cannot look to a single regime and decide, 'Let's do it their way.'

In addition, PISA tests do not provide a comprehensive overview of the successes and failures of any single education system. For that, we need to consider many other factors, such as the proportion of young people not in education, employment or training after the age of 16; the proportion of people who hold higher level qualifications; adult rates of employment; measures of economic productivity; and so on. The point is that no single measure tells us *everything* about the success of a country's education system, but all of them are capable of telling us *something*.

With that in mind, let us turn to two case studies, Austria and Ontario.

Austria

Austria achieves broadly average results in PISA tests, so it is not mentioned in the same breath as Singapore or Finland.

But on many other measures of success – not least, the strength of the economy – Austria seems to be doing something right. In particular, a lasting commitment to technical and vocational education has undoubtedly been a source of enormous strength for well over 100 years.

In Austria, compulsory education starts in the September following a child's sixth birthday. Primary education lasts four years (Grades 1 to 4). Secondary education is subdivided into level 1 and level 2. Level 1 covers Grades 5 to 8 (age 10 to 14). From the age of 10, most children attend the lower cycle of an *Allgeneinbildende hörere Schule* (academic secondary school) or a *Hauptshule* (general school).

Entry to an academic secondary school at age 10 is based on ability, particularly in German, reading and mathematics. The curriculum is very largely academic, and is intended to prepare young people for university. From the third year, students are able to exercise a degree of choice: for example, they may learn a second modern language or Latin; commit more time to science subjects; or choose additional instruction in a technical subject.

In the general secondary school, pupils are grouped by ability in German, mathematics and modern foreign languages. The top set follows a curriculum similar to the academic secondary school. In all other subjects, mixed-ability teaching is the norm.

During secondary level 1, the general secondary school curriculum is largely similar to that taught in the academic secondary school. However, a certain number of general secondary schools have additional specialisms such as music, sport and skiing.

There has been growing concern about academic selection at age 10. Mirroring debates in England in the 1950s and 1960s, parents and teachers have started to question whether it is realistic to divide children as young as 10 into 'academic' sheep and 'technical' goats. There is a widespread belief that talents and ambitions are unclear at that age, and that it would be better to facilitate informed choice at 14 instead.

This has led to the establishment of 320 new middle schools (*Neue Mittelschule*). Again, they cater for pupils aged 10–14. All have been created since 2008, very largely by converting existing general secondary schools: only 11 were previously academic secondary schools (OECD, 2011a). Although (again) the curriculum is similar to that taught in academic secondary schools, all subjects are taught in mixed-ability classes.

Middle schools emphasize new styles of learning (e.g. cross-curricular projects and experiential learning) and personal qualities such as creativity, teamwork and independence. In the words of the Federal Ministry for Education (2009):

Starting from their individual potential, pupils will be supported and their performance advanced in every possible way. Apart from adjusting teaching programmes to children's individual learning rates, the emphasis is on exploratory learning, self-learning and practice-oriented learning. Further core themes are integration, equality of opportunity and gender equality, advancement in the areas of creativity, sports, and e-learning as well as all-day support and supervision and the opening up of schools to the outside world.

As noted already, a key aim of the new middle schools is to delay 'tracking' students onto academic or vocational pathways. Based on achievement and preferences at the end of Grade 8, therefore, middle school students are able to move on to an academic secondary school or to a medium- or high-level technical and vocational school.

Secondary level 2

At 14, some young Austrians stay on at their academic or general secondary school and study mainly academic subjects in preparation for direct entry to university. In some areas of the country, there is a further type of academic school, the *Oberstufenrealgymnasium*, which provides academic education for Grades 9 to 12.

However, around 80 per cent of all young people choose a *technical or vocational* pathway at some point after their fourteenth birthday. Various types of schools provide opportunities for them, such as the *Höhere Technische Lehranstalten* (higher technical institute), *Berufsbildende Höhere Schule* (vocational high school) and the *Berufsbildende Mittlere Schule* (secondary vocational school).

Students who enrol at technical and vocational schools follow full-time programmes lasting up to four years in medium-level schools and up to five years in high-level schools, with the latter offering clear pathways to university. Each school has one or more specialism, ranging from interior design to ICT and from art and design to electrical engineering. In all cases, students follow a general education for one-third of the time, with vocational theory and practice making up the other two-thirds. Specialization increases as students progress. Technical subjects are taught in workshops or other well-equipped facilities (e.g. training kitchens) by people with relevant industrial or commercial experience. Local businesses are represented on school boards.

Over recent years, there has been a growing emphasis on cross-curricular teaching and group projects in technical and vocational schools. In addition, many schools encourage students to develop skills for enterprise by setting up 'training firms' along the lines of the Young Enterprise company scheme in the United Kingdom. The ministry for education describes a training firm as a 'mock-up' or model of a real-life company, where the operational procedures of actual companies are reproduced to varying levels of complexity. More than 70 per cent of the training firms have links with local businesses, which offer advice and support (Federal Ministry for Education, Arts and Culture, 2011).

Pre-vocational schools provide a combination of general education, basic vocational training and vocational guidance and orientation. Compulsory subjects include German, a modern foreign language, maths, religious education and physical education. Vocational options link to major sectors of the economy. Vocational guidance and orientation includes support for skills for employment and life.

About 40 per cent of all young Austrians take up an apprenticeship in one of nearly 250 registered trades. *Berufsschule* – compulsory vocational schools – support the 'dual system' of apprenticeship and part-time education. Attendance is linked to the length of the apprenticeship and can last between two and four years. The curriculum includes general subjects such as German and a modern foreign language (taught in the context of the apprentice's occupation), as well as background knowledge linked to specific apprenticeships.

The success of technical and vocational education in Austria

The success of technical and vocational education is a source of considerable pride in Austria. Indeed, in September 2011 the Minister for Education, Claudia Schmied, declared: 'Topping OECD and EU rankings, we are "world champions" in vocational education. This is a key factor behind Austria's low youth unemployment, which is the envy of many countries' (Federal Chancellery, 2011).

This is borne out in the statistics. In 2011, EU figures showed that across 27 member states, 16.7 per cent of young people aged 18–24 were NEET. In the United Kingdom, the figure was slightly higher – 18.4 per cent – but in Austria, it was very much lower – 8.4 per cent (Eurostat, 2012). In addition, the average young Austrian finds work less than 6 months after leaving education; the average across 12 other European countries is nearer 17 months (Hoeckel, 2010, p. 14).

Austria also has a strong economy. In 2011, output is estimated to have grown by 3.1 per cent, significantly above the EU average of 1.5 per cent (European Union, 2012). The strength of the economy, low rates of youth unemployment and high standards of technical and vocational education are undoubtedly connected: a highly skilled workforce makes a significant contribution to Austria's economic and social success (OECD, 2011b).

Ontario, Canada

In Canada, education policy is established at the level of the ten provinces and three territories. Ontario performs consistently well in PISA reading, maths and science tests, with results very close to the Canadian average (Education Quality and Accountability Office, 2010). For this reason, it was chosen as one of twelve countries and jurisdictions to be examined as part of the review of the National Curriculum in England (National Foundation for Educational Research, 2011).

Education in Ontario consists of two phases: elementary (age 6–14) and secondary (age 14–18). Province-wide tests in literacy, numeracy, science and history provide teachers and parents with evidence of each student's progress. The current curriculum dates back to 2000, and since 2008, education has been compulsory for all young people up to the age of 18: previously, compulsory education ended at 16.

Students work towards high school graduation by achieving credits in a range of core and optional subjects. A credit is granted on the successful completion of a course scheduled to last at least 110 hours. (For comparison, a GCSE generally takes 120 guided learning hours.) 'Successful' means a passmark of 50 per cent or higher.

In order to graduate from high school with an Ontario Secondary School Diploma, students must achieve the following compulsory credits:

Compulsory credits	Plus one credit from each of the following groups		
	Group 1	Group 2	Group 3
4 credits in English: one credit per grade (school year)	English	health and physical education	science (in Grade 11 or 12)
	French as a second language		technological education
3 credits in maths (one of which must be achieved in Grade 11 or 12)	a Native language	the arts	French as a second language
	a classical or international language	business studies	
2 credits in science		French as a second language	computer studies
1 credit in Canadian history	social sciences and the humanities	cooperative education	cooperative education
1 credit in Canadian geography	Canadian and world studies		
1 credit in the arts			
1 credit in health and physical education	guidance and career education		
1 credit in French as a second language	cooperative education (i.e. a combination of work-based learning and classroom study)		
0.5 credit in career studies			
0.5 credit in civics			

Note: This is the list for students whose mother tongue is English; there are rules of combination limiting the choice of additional credits in groups 1, 2 and 3.

In addition, students must complete 12 optional credits, 40 hours of community involvement and pass the provincial literacy test.

Students normally aim to complete 16 credits in Grades 9 and 10 (age 14–16) and the remaining 14 in Years 11 and 12 (age 16–18). Students who have not completed all 30 credits by the end of Grade 12 may stay on at high school for a further year. Alternatively students may qualify for the Ontario Secondary School Certificate, which is awarded on request to students aged 18 who have achieved a minimum of 14 credits (Ontario Ministry of Education, 2010).

Many of the optional credits are offered in bundles of 8–10 courses under the title, 'Specialist High Skills Majors'. In the 2011–12 school year, SHSMs are available in the following sectors (Ontario Ministry of Education, 2011):

- Agriculture
- Arts and Culture
- Aviation/Aerospace
- Business
- Construction
- Energy
- Environment
- Forestry
- Health and Wellness
- Horticulture and Landscaping
- Hospitality and Tourism
- Information and Communications Technology
- Justice, Community Safety and Emergency Services
- Manufacturing
- Mining
- Non-profit
- Sports
- Transportation.

The SHSM provides a menu of options for students, including those who are unenthusiastic about a purely academic curriculum. Working with employers also helps students see how education leads, directly or indirectly, to employment opportunities (OECD, 2010c).

A further option, a dual credit programme, exists for students who want to earn high school credits while studying at a local college or taking apprenticeship training. This bears similarities to the dual system in Austria.

Ontario's approach is clearly successful – PISA and other international benchmarks tell us so. However, that is not the only measure of success. For example – and very significantly – high school graduation rates have risen rapidly since the Ontario Curriculum was introduced, from 68 per cent in 2003–4 to 81 per cent in 2009–10 (Government of Ontario, 2011). Post-compulsory education rates have risen, too, to the extent that Ontario is near the top of the OECD league table for post-secondary enrolment rates (OECD, 2010c, p. 3).

Conclusion

The English curriculum should take account of our own heritage, traditions and priorities. Nevertheless, we can learn from both Austria – with its new interest in general education up to age 14 and choice of pathways thereafter – and Ontario, whose credit-based post-14 curriculum takes maximum advantage of a four-year programme of learning to provide *both* a sound basic education *and* a choice of specialist learning.

SUMMARY OF RECOMMENDATIONS

1. The National Curriculum should cover the ages 5–14.

2. There should be three phases of education: primary, middle and secondary, covering ages 5–8, 9–13 and 14–18. The first two phases could be combined on a single campus for ages 5–14 or provided by separate institutions.

3. 14–18 colleges should provide four pathways for students:

   a. University Technical College

   b. Liberal Arts College

   c. Sports, Creative and Performing Arts College

   d. Career College

4. At the age of 14, young people should select which pathway they wish to follow, taking account of the following:

   a. their own talents, interests and ambitions

   b. the advice of their parents and teachers

   c. information about how their choices will affect future learning opportunities (e.g. further and higher education and apprenticeships) and careers.

5. All 14–18 colleges should provide teaching in English, maths, science, a foreign language and history or geography. Existing statutory requirements covering religious and physical education (for example) should be respected. The teaching time allotted

to these core and statutory subjects should amount to about 60 per cent of the teaching day for 14–16-year-olds.

6. The remaining 40 per cent of 14–16 teaching time should be devoted to optional, specialist subjects (e.g. engineering or performing arts). All young people should experience 'learning by doing' as part of a balanced curriculum, and business, financial and entrepreneurial skills should be woven into the curriculum to improve students' employability.

7. The teaching day should be extended to 8 hours on most days of the week, and the number of teaching weeks should be extended from 38 to 40.

8. Post-16, young people should spend at least 60 per cent of the teaching day on their chosen specialist subjects. However, they should continue to have access to core subjects including English and maths, with an emphasis on how they are used in the chosen specialist area. Similarly, they should continue to develop business, financial and entrepreneurial skills, and the 'soft' skills demanded by employers – teamwork, problem-solving and so on.

9. Universities should help to design the curriculum for each pathway, to ensure that potentially, any young person might progress to HE (including degree-level apprenticeship), regardless of their chosen pathway. At a local level, universities should help 14–18 colleges through visits, projects, student teaching and student–pupil mentoring.

10. Local employers should be engaged actively in the preparation of the specialist curriculum, and in providing teaching modules and team projects. Employers, their staff and apprentices should be encouraged to support middle schools and 14–18 colleges by acting as mentors, discussing careers and getting involved in hands-on projects.

11. The FE sector should be separated into two distinct activities – one for the age group 14–18 and the other, post-18. The 14–18 sector, which should be answerable to the Department for Education, should establish Career Colleges as separate Academies: these should be supported by a university and local

employers and cover a wide range of vocational subjects such as catering, hospitality, fashion, hair and beauty, tourism and the caring services, but specializing in no more than two. They should offer YAs for 14–16-year-olds and full apprenticeships for students aged 16 and over. The post-18 sector should be reorganized to provide new polytechnics and be responsible to the Department for Business, Innovation and Skills.

12. A range of worthwhile qualifications should be established, fully equivalent to academic subjects at GCSE and A-level, but taken when each student is ready, not at an arbitrary, fixed point. Over the four years from 14–18, students should accumulate credits towards an overarching graduation certificate.

13. The success of education should be measured not only on the basis of exam results and international tests of English, maths and science skills, but also on the proportion of young people who succeed in finding work after completing their education. Lessons should be learned from those countries which have low rates of youth unemployment as well as from those which do well in international tests.

14. These proposals have significant implications for the school estate. However, the school population is set to grow significantly over the next decade or more, and from 2015, all young people will be legally required to remain in education or training until they are 18. This will provide the perfect opportunity to reconfigure schools to support the vision of three-tier education and four pathways from 14 to 18. This will parallel the growth in the number of middle schools in the 1970s, which reflected rising pupil numbers, the raising of the school leaving age and the widespread introduction of comprehensive education.

APPENDIX 1
TECHNICAL SECONDARY EDUCATION IN ENGLAND: A BRIEF HISTORY

David Harbourne

The nineteenth-century origins of technical secondary education

Most of the nineteenth-century secondary schools were what we now call 'public schools' and 'grammar schools'. Most of their pupils were the sons of wealthy parents. The curriculum was heavily influenced by the work of Dr Thomas Arnold, headmaster of Rugby School from 1828 to 1841. Lytton Strachey noted that although Arnold 'introduced modern history, modern languages, and mathematics into the school curriculum . . . The boys' main study remained the dead languages of Greece and Rome' (Strachey, 1918). Indeed, the physical sciences – chemistry, physics and biology – were not taught at all during Arnold's time at Rugby.

In short, the curriculum offered by nineteenth-century public and grammar schools was not remotely concerned with 'technical' education.

Nor was it 'vocational', except in the sense that it helped prepare young men for careers in law, medicine and public administration at home or elsewhere in the British empire. Furthermore, very few children stayed at school beyond the age of 12.

Gradually, however, concerns were expressed that Britain was starting to fall behind its industrial competitors. One reason was said to be a failure to educate and train young people for careers in engineering or other branches of industry. These concerns were summed up in the 1938 Spens Report:

> The development of public interest in technical education . . . was largely due to the pressure of foreign competition. At the Great Exhibition held in London in 1851 there were 100 departments in which goods were displayed, and in most of these Great Britain was awarded the prize. At the Paris Exhibition of 1867 there were 90 departments, and Great Britain received prizes in only 10 of these. British firms which exhibited at the Exhibition at Paris in 1878 had similar experiences, and public opinion at last began to be impressed by the inadequacy of the provision for technical education. (Board of Education, 1938, pp. 51–2)

This led to the appointment of a Royal Commission on Technical Instruction, which published its final report in 1884. On the subject of secondary and technical instruction, the Commission recommended the following (among other things):

a That provision be made by the Charity Commissioners for the establishment, in suitable localities, of schools or departments of schools, in which the study of natural science, drawing, mathematics, and modern languages shall take the place of Latin and Greek.

b That local authorities be empowered, if they think fit, to establish, maintain, and contribute to the establishment and maintenance of secondary and technical (including agricultural) schools and colleges. (House of Commons, 1884)

Within the following few years, higher grade schools, organized science schools and technical day schools were set up in many parts of the country. In addition, a number of post-secondary technical institutes and colleges were established.

Higher grade schools were an interesting experiment in technical secondary education. They offered extended education to children aged 11 and over, at a time when the vast majority of children left school at 12. By 1890, there were around 400 higher grade schools in England. Normal hours were 9 to 5, 44 weeks of the year.

Although the education offered by higher grade schools was free of charge, there was – quite clearly – an opportunity cost: parents had to pay for their children's upkeep, and of course the children concerned earned no wages while they were still at school. Education at the higher grade schools therefore had to have a clear value. Parents – who mostly belonged to the working and lower-middle classes – expected their children to achieve measurable results.

Against this background, higher grade schools pioneered a new type of curriculum for both boys and girls, which Meriel Vlaeminke described as:

useful but not narrowly utilitarian, combining practical, technical, intellectual, cultural, physical and aesthetic pursuits . . . heads were happy to accept the paramount duty of educating children for 'the practical needs of afterlife', but passionately argued their right to access to literary culture and to 'knowledge of their own glorious inheritance'. (Vlaeminke, 1990, p. 60. Quotations in this passage are drawn from contemporary reports in *The Schoolmaster.*)

On leaving higher grade schools, pupils found work in many fields, including civil, mechanical and electrical engineering, surveying, dyeworks, factories, chemical works, architects' offices, art rooms and design studios.

Higher grade schools entered pupils for exams offered by a range of examining bodies. The most prominent was the Science and Art Department, which was initially dedicated largely to science and technical education. During the 1890s, its remit expanded to encourage a broad curriculum including English, maths and foreign languages.

Early twentieth century: the tide turns against technical secondary education

Technical education such as provided by higher grade schools was not universally popular. The tide turned decisively against technical secondary education in 1902, when Robert Morant was appointed permanent secretary of the Board of Education. He strongly favoured the classical and literary curriculum taught in public schools and grammar schools.

Against this background, the Board of Education passed new Secondary Regulations in 1904 which required pupils in secondary schools to study the following:

a English language and literature;

b geography and history;

c at least one language other than English;

d mathematics and science, both theoretical and practical;

e drawing.

For girls, 'Practical Housewifery' was to be included as well; and for both boys and girls some provision was required for 'Manual Work' and 'Physical Exercises' (Gillard, 2011). However, technical education as developed by higher grade schools was not included in the new regulations.

As a result of Morant's policies, many higher grade schools dropped technical education. Others closed altogether. A senior official at the Board of Education commented on one such case, 'I think we may now congratulate ourselves on having extinguished the exceedingly unsatisfactory Walsall Municipal Technical Day School' (quoted by Vlaeminke, 1990, p. 70).

The grammar school curriculum had very largely prevailed, as Morant intended. It was adopted by the many new secondary schools opened in the years following the First World War, further reinforced by the School Examination Regulations of 1917 which prescribed the external exams which pupils could take: namely, the School Certificate (at age 16) and Higher School Certificate (at age 18). In order to pass the School Certificate, a candidate had to demonstrate reasonable attainment in each of three groups of subjects: (1) English, (2) languages and (3) science and maths. The aims were first, to test the results of a course of general education and second, to prepare and qualify pupils for admission to university or the professions. Furthermore, the second aim rapidly overtook the first in terms of perceived importance.

The 1930s and 1940s: the second rise of technical education

Despite the immense influence of the grammar school curriculum, secondary technical education did not disappear entirely in the early decades of the twentieth century. A number of local education authorities found ways of circumventing the secondary regulations by establishing new technical schools for children who had completed their elementary education (i.e. children aged 13+). These technical schools came in many different guises, including junior technical schools, junior commercial schools, junior art schools and trade schools. By 1938, there were 248 technical schools, attended by 30,457 pupils. Very few had more than 200 pupils; most had fewer than 100. Around 85 per cent were junior departments of technical colleges, often sharing some of their more specialized facilities. In addition, selective central schools were set up in London, Birmingham, Manchester, Leeds and Bradford, which provided a significant element of practical learning in the curriculum (Bailey, 1990).

In the 1930s, there was a growing interest in technical education as a high-quality alternative to a conventional academic curriculum. This led to the Spens Report, 'Secondary Education with Special Reference to Grammar Schools and Technical High Schools', the product of a five-year inquiry chaired by William Spens.

The Committee's report, published in 1938, strongly criticized the Board of Education for failing to promote technical and vocational secondary education:

Perhaps the most striking feature of the new Secondary Schools provided by local education authorities, which have so greatly increased in numbers since 1902, is their marked disinclination to deviate to any considerable extent from the main lines of the traditional grammar school curriculum. . . . We cannot but deplore the fact that the Board [of Education] did little or nothing . . . to foster the development of secondary schools of quasi-vocational type designed to meet the needs of boys and girls who desired to enter industry and commerce at the age of 16. (Board of Education, 1938, pp. 71–2)

The report recommended that new technical schools should be created alongside grammar schools. The Committee also recommended that the school leaving age should be raised to 15, and that modern schools should cater for those pupils who did not find places at a grammar or technical school.

Further progress was delayed by the outbreak of the Second World War. Nevertheless, the Board of Education started planning for post-war educational reconstruction as early as 1940 and the following year, the president of the Board of Education invited Sir Cyril Norwood to chair a Committee to consider the secondary school curriculum and future structure of examinations.

The Norwood Report was published in 1943. It endorsed the notion of a tripartite approach to secondary education, stating that for practical reasons, 'school organisation and class instruction must assume that individuals have enough in common as regards capacities and interests to justify certain rough groupings' (Board of Education, 1943, p. 2). Based on a division of pupils into three broad 'groupings', Norwood proposed three types of secondary curriculum. The first was essentially the long-established grammar school curriculum. Norwood proposed that the second, technical curriculum

would be closely, though not wholly, directed to the special data and skills associated with a particular kind of occupation; its outlook and its methods would always be bounded by a near horizon clearly envisaged. It would thus be closely related to industry, trades and commerce in all their diversity. (Board of Education, 1943, p. 4)

The third type of curriculum would 'enable pupils to take up the work of life' through the training of both mind and body (Board of Education, 1943, p. 4).

The Education Act of 1944 permitted, but did not require, the establishment of this three-tier structure of secondary education. Local authorities were given considerable discretion: they were required to submit proposals for reorganizing secondary education in their areas, but the Act did not specify what these plans should look like. Some wholeheartedly embraced Norwood's vision and established a tripartite model comprising separate grammar, technical and modern schools. Others preferred an essentially two-tier approach (grammar and secondary modern), while others developed bilateral and multilateral schools which combined two or three streams (grammar, technical and/ or modern) in a single set of buildings.

It was hoped that modern testing techniques would make it easy to assess the aptitudes of children at the age of 11 so that they could be guided towards the 'right' kind of school. In practice, it proved virtually impossible to differentiate between pupils likely to thrive in a grammar school and those likely to thrive in a technical school. In *The Secondary Technical School*, published in 1960, Reese Edwards concluded that 'What both the secondary grammar school and the secondary technical school . . . require is exactly the same, namely boys who can think' (Edwards, 1960, p. 69).

Placed in a difficult position, most local education authorities with technical schools took the line of least resistance, directing the most able pupils to grammar schools, the next in order of ability to technical schools, and the rest to modern schools.

Post-war technical schools

In 1945, the majority of technical schools were the pre-war junior technical schools, junior commercial schools and trade schools, which had been redesignated but not reformed, and they recruited at 13 or 14, not at 11.

The first entirely new secondary technical school opened in 1949. In the 10 years to 1957, a total of 57 new technical schools opened. A few more followed, but it was hardly a flood. And when Reese Edwards visited 200 technical schools at the end of the 1950s, he found that 98 *still* had an entrance age of 13+. He also wrote:

There is no doubt that the standard of buildings which have been used for secondary technical school purposes is considerably lower than the standards of buildings used for either secondary grammar, secondary modern, primary or nursery school purposes. (Edwards, 1960, p. 34)

Reese Edwards was – nevertheless – able to report some remarkable success stories. It is clear that staff in many technical schools worked hard to help their pupils succeed.

However, the statistics show that technical schools – indeed, technical education as a whole – failed to develop strongly in the years following the 1944 Education Act. In 1957–8, when 97,485 pupils were taking technical school courses, 608,034 were taking grammar school courses; these formed part of a total secondary school population of 2,331,063 (Edwards, 1960, p. 186). In other words, technical courses were being taken by only 4 per cent of all secondary school pupils.

By the time Edwards' book was published in 1960, the number of technical schools was already starting to fall. In 1954–5, there had been 302; by 1957–8, there were 279. The end was in sight.

Secondary modern schools

A significant number of new secondary modern schools opened during the 1950s. Headteachers often spoke optimistically about the evolution of modern schools. The head of Ellis Secondary School for Boys in Nottingham, described how his school had transformed the curriculum:

> The 14-year-olds [in my school] were plainly bored. If we took out the few 'A' intelligences, who in any event found a gainful occupation, and the lower 'C' stream, who with a dull contentment mowed the lawns and weeded the rockery, we were left with a mass in the middle straining at the bonds that tied them to the school desk.

> For the 13's to 15's I [therefore] planned two-year courses under each of these headings – Power Supplies, Transport and Communications, Raw Materials, Public Services and Social History. (Hadrill, 1955)

However, this vision of a reformed curriculum was the exception, not the rule. The Newsom Report, 'Half Our Future', which acknowledged the work of many good secondary modern schools, stated:

> [M]ost of the distinctive courses which have proved so successful have, for understandable historical reasons, so far been designed for the abler pupils. It would be idle to pretend that all the rest of the pupils are satisfied or satisfactory customers. Too many at present seem to sit through lessons with information and exhortation washing over them and leaving very little deposit. Too many appear to be bored and apathetic in school, as some will be in their jobs also. Others are openly impatient. They 'don't see the point' of what they are asked to do. (Ministry of Education, 1963, p. 14)

More significantly, schools offering these additional opportunities were in the minority. The report includes a summary of the fourth year (Year 10) curriculum in a typical secondary modern school, expressed as a percentage of time given to each group of subjects. This is illustrated in Table A.1.

Table A.1 The use of time in the fourth year of a typical secondary modern school (percentage of time spent on subject areas)

	Boys (%)	Girls (%)
Humanities (English, religious instruction, history, geography, etc.)	39	39
Science and mathematics	24	22
Practical subjects – of which	37	39
– Art and music	9	13
– Physical education	10	8
– Woodwork and metalwork	12	–
– Technical drawing	6	–
– Housecraft and needlework	–	18

Source: Ministry of Education (1963), diagram 13, p. 237.

It is clear from Table A.1 that the most obviously vocational subjects – woodwork, metalwork, technical drawing and needlework – occupied a small percentage of the fourth-form curriculum in the average secondary modern school.

The Newsom Report recommended a large-scale expansion in vocationally biased courses:

> We are convinced not only that such courses should be more widely available in all areas – and this implies adequate facilities for them, which many schools at present do not possess – but also that many of the less gifted pupils would respond to comparable opportunities.

> We suggest that for by far the majority of our pupils, courses will need to have a substantial craft or practical element, with an emphasis on real tasks undertaken with adult equipment. (Ministry of Education, 1963, p. 34)

Newsom's recommendations were never fully implemented. Reasons included the sheer cost of providing new, specialist facilities in economically challenging times; the slow move towards a comprehensive education system; and in some ways most significant of all, shortages of teachers with the right skills, qualifications and experience.

The 1960s: the tide turns against secondary technical education (again)

In 1959, the Crowther Report noted that 'more and more people are coming to believe that it is wrong to label children for all time at 11' (Ministry of Education, 1959, p. 23). Indeed, some local authorities started to establish comprehensive schools years before the Department of Education and Science issued Circular 10/65, which firmly established twin objectives: to end selection at 11+ and eliminate separatism in secondary education (Department of Education and Science, 1965).

From the 1960s onwards, therefore, technical schools were gradually transformed into comprehensive schools, merged with other schools or closed entirely. To the extent that comprehensive schools offered technical or vocational options, these were very largely based on what they inherited from secondary modern schools – woodwork, metalwork, domestic science and so on. Interest in secondary technical and vocational education subsided, resurfacing once more only in the mid-1970s.

Meanwhile, there was a pressing need to increase the supply of teachers, and the number of university places for would-be teachers increased rapidly after the publication of the Robbins Report on HE in 1963. One effect was that the number of teachers with prior experience of other types of employment dwindled; as they retired, they were replaced by teachers arriving straight from university, where they had (in the main) studied mainstream academic subjects. The number of teachers with the skills and experience to teach technical and vocational subjects fell as older teachers retired, including many who had learned skills (e.g. in engineering) during the Second World War, or as part of their national service.

The 1970s and 1980s: a tug of war

In 1976, Prime Minister James Callaghan made a famous speech at Ruskin College. He said he had heard

> complaints from industry that new recruits from the schools sometimes do not have the basic tools to do the job that is required. . . . I have [also] been concerned to find out that many of our best trained students who have completed the higher levels of education at university or polytechnic have no desire to join industry. Their preferences are to stay in academic life or to find their way into the civil service. There seems to be a need for more technological bias in science teaching that will lead towards practical applications in industry rather than towards academic studies.

The Ruskin speech launched what became known as the Great Debate, prompting renewed interest in the curriculum across the political spectrum.

In 1981, the Conservative government published advice to local education authorities on curriculum development, 'The School Curriculum', which summed up the state of the secondary curriculum in these terms:

> At present, for the first three years in most secondary schools pupils follow broadly similar programmes. These generally include English, mathematics, science, history, geography, religious education, art, music, home economics, craft design and technology, physical education and games. Nearly all pupils also embark on a foreign language, usually French.
>
> In the fourth and fifth years, the number of subjects studied by all pupils is much reduced. Some subjects are dropped, others added, with varying degrees of guidance and control. The result is that a balanced curriculum for each individual pupil is not always assured. (Department of Education and Science, 1981, p. 13)

The definition of a 'balanced curriculum' included English, maths, science, religious education and physical education. For the first time, too, the government stressed the importance of learning about computers. Modern languages should be studied by most pupils. In addition, pupils should undertake some study of the humanities and have time for 'practical and aesthetic activity':

> The Secretaries of State attach special importance to craft, design and technology as a part of the preparation for living and working in modern industrial society. . . . It encourages creative skills and the ability to identify, examine and solve problems, using a variety of materials. The problems tackled by able pupils are intellectually demanding and stretch to the full their inventive and innovative powers. (Department of Education and Science, 1981, p. 17)

More generally,

> The curriculum needs to be related to what happens outside schools. As schools and examination boards have increasingly acknowledged in recent years, the curriculum needs to include more applied and practical work, particularly in science and mathematics; and pupils

need to be given a better understanding of the economic base of our society and the importance to Britain of the wealth creating process. (Department of Education and Science, 1981, p. 18)

In some respects, therefore, the government appeared to be pulling in two different directions. On the one hand, young people were expected to follow a broad curriculum up to the age of 16; on the other, there was a renewed interest in technical subjects and links with the world of work. This tug of war reached a new peak in the 1980s, with the quite separate development of the Technical and Vocational Education Initiative (TVEI) by the Manpower Services Commission and the National Curriculum by the Department for Education and Science.

The TVEI

In 1982, the government announced a new TVEI for young people aged 14–18. TVEI marked a major departure from previous practice, not least because it was run by the Manpower Services Commission under the supervision of the Department for Employment, and not by the Department for Education and Science.

The initiative was the brainchild of the chairman of the Manpower Services Commission, David Young (later Lord Young of Graffham). In his autobiography, *The Enterprise Years*, he writes about TVEI under the heading 'Dawn Raid on Education'. His original idea was to open a network of technical schools for young people aged 14–18:

I suggested to Keith [Joseph, secretary of state for education] that we open a series of technical schools around the country. 'Let them be outside the existing state system if we have to', I suggested . . . 'Let them succeed', I said, 'and we will infect the system. Then they will all want to change.' (Young, 1990, p. 96)

In the event, the notion of new technical schools was used only as a threat: if the educational establishment did not support plans for a new vocational curriculum, Young would go ahead and open new schools.

Local education authorities proved keen to support TVEI, and pilot projects were up and running by early 1983. TVEI was made more widely available from 1984. Young wrote:

> Each [pilot] project provided for 250 entrants at fourteen, and then an annual intake of 250 pupils until the full complement of 1,000 per project was achieved. The individual applications showed a great deal of variety and there was no doubt that we had captured the imagination of many teachers. Many of the projects found new and imaginative ways to bring schools and colleges of further education together for the very first time. But they would not be technical schools.
>
> . . . Slowly, carefully and painfully we agreed the way ahead. We had to make some compromises but the package we ended up with was far more realistic and vocational than anything that had existed up to now in the school system. (Young, 1990, pp. 102–3)

In this pilot phase:

> [TVEI] was intended to develop dedicated pathways of largely vocational education for non-academic, but far from 'problem' young people – according to David Young, the chairman of the Manpower Service Commission which was charged with introducing it – for the 'the 15 to 85 percentiles of the ability range' (quoted in Chitty, 1989). Programmes would stretch from 14 until 18, thus erecting a distinctly vocational track. (West and Steedman, 2003, p. 8)

However, TVEI rapidly moved away from this aim. David Young left the MSC, Keith Joseph left the Department for Education and Norman Tebbitt left the Department for Employment. These three had had a powerful influence over TVEI and once they moved on, the original aims were watered down; in its later stages, the overarching purpose of TVEI was to relate everything learned in schools and colleges to the world of work. TVEI finally ended in 1997.

The National Curriculum

The National Curriculum was introduced in 1988. Straddling primary and secondary education, the National Curriculum was structured around the following subjects:

- English
- Maths
- Science
- Art and design
- Design and technology
- Geography
- History
- ICT
- Music
- Physical education.

Although technically outside the National Curriculum, schools were also required to teach religious education. At Key Stage 3, pupils also studied citizenship and a modern foreign language.

The National Curriculum did not require vocational education to be provided in secondary schools. However, schools were free to offer technical and vocational courses to students aged 14+, provided they also delivered the full National Curriculum.

Vocational Qualifications

GNVQs were introduced in 1993 partly in response to curriculum pressures and partly as a way of linking school-based qualifications with the new suite of work-based NVQs. They were criticized as unwieldy, especially in the early stages: in 1995, this led to the appointment of a committee, chaired by John Capey, to review the assessment and grading of GNVQs.

Nevertheless, GNVQs became reasonably popular alternatives to GCSEs and A-levels. Take-up was highest in business, health and social care, art and design and leisure and tourism. However, there was a strong emphasis on learning and writing *about* the subject matter as opposed to learning to *do* things (Pring et al., 2009, p. 69). The explicitly vocational content was minimal, and many courses were taught by people with little or no industrial or commercial experience.

GNVQs were also intended to raise the prestige of vocational qualifications. The phrase, 'parity of esteem' had been used for many years in debates about raising the status of vocational education, and it was hoped that GNVQs would enjoy the same status as GCSEs and A-Levels. They didn't. Like other vocational qualifications before and since, they were generally regarded as best suited to young people who might struggle with academic subjects. The Advanced GNVQ was therefore replaced in 2000 by Advanced Vocational Certificates of Education (AVCEs), which fared little better.

The early twentieth century: renewed interest in technical and vocational education

The Labour government published a schools white paper in 2001. One chapter was devoted to the concept of a 14–19 'phase' of education. Reviewing the challenges, the white paper noted that only 73 per cent of UK 17-year-olds were enrolled in education, compared with an OECD average of 82 per cent, and participation rates of 90 per cent or higher in countries such as France, Germany and Japan. In addition, it was claimed that 'The secondary curriculum, particularly post-14, can seem crowded and to some pupils lacking in interest and relevance. It is arguable that there is too little flexibility in the curriculum to meet and bring out individual aptitudes, abilities and preferences' (Department for Education and Skills, 2001, p. 14).

The white paper went on to say:

> A well balanced 14–19 phase of learning is crucial if we are to achieve our objective of well-motivated young people playing their full part in society and in the economy, and that this 14–19 phase would –
>
> - Recognize achievement in both academic and vocational subjects, perhaps through an overarching award
>
> - Create space in the 14–16 curriculum to allow students to pursue their talents and aspirations, while maintaining a strong focus on the basics
>
> - Make high quality vocational options available to all students, which are widely recognised and offer the opportunity of entry to Higher Education. (Department for Education and Skills, 2001, p. 30)

The idea of the overarching award was further developed by a Working Group on 14–19 Reform chaired by Sir Mike Tomlinson (Department for Education and Skills, 2004). In 2004, the Working Group recommended the introduction of diplomas at 4 levels (entry, foundation, intermediate and advanced), and in 20 'lines of learning'. These would include both academic and vocational disciplines.

In the event, the government was unwilling to risk such a far-reaching reform, not least because it would (in effect) replace A-levels, still widely regarded as the 'gold standard' of English education. Instead, the government announced in 2005 that a suite of sector-related Diplomas would be developed to run *alongside* GCSEs, A-levels and other 14–19 qualifications (Department for Education and Skills, 2005). The government intended that there should be four qualification pathways: general (GCSEs and A-levels), Diplomas, apprenticeships and foundation learning (i.e. programmes below level 2).

In the meantime, however, the government had introduced new flexibility into the Key Stage 4 curriculum (age 14–16). From 2004, several subject areas including design and technology and modern foreign languages became entitlements rather than requirements. In the same year, schools were required to provide young people with work-related learning during Key Stage 4.

As a result, schools were able to offer a much wider choice of Key Stage 4 subjects and qualifications, including BTECs and OCR Nationals linked to particular sectors of the economy, and qualifications intended to develop broader social and 'employability' skills, such as ASDAN awards. These became known as VRQs.

For the purposes of school accountability, many VRQs were deemed to be equivalent to more than one GCSE. Critics claimed this led schools to offer them to boost their position in the school league tables, rather than (necessarily or solely) because they were in the best interests of individual students; in due course, this criticism led to the Wolf Review of Vocational Education (Wolf, 2011).

Figures prepared by the Department for Education for the Wolf Review show that the number of Level 1 and 2 VRQs achieved at the end of Key Stage 4 rose from 12,889 in 2004 to 587,549 in 2010 (Wolf, 2011, p. 47). They effectively supplanted GNVQs and almost all Applied GCSEs, and made it very difficult for Diplomas – which were taught for the first time in the 2008–9 academic year – to find a place in the curriculum of most schools.

2010: the coalition government

In May 2010, a coalition government took office. Secretary of State for Education Michael Gove promised an array of reforms and published a white paper *The Importance of Teaching* in November 2010. In a statement to the House of Commons, he said:

> We will slim down a curriculum which has become over-loaded, over-prescriptive and over-bureaucratic by stripping out unnecessary clutter and simply specifying the core knowledge in strategic subjects which every child should know at each key stage. (HC Hansard, vol. 519, col. 268, 24 November 2010)

The white paper also proposed:

> [A] new award – the English Baccalaureate – for any student who secures good GCSE or iGCSE passes in English, mathematics, the sciences, a modern or ancient foreign language and a humanity such as history or geography. (Department for Education, 2010, p. 44)

In September 2012, the government took the further step of proposing that GCSEs in EBac subjects should be replaced by individual English Baccalaureate Certificates.

On the topic of vocational qualifications, the white paper said:

[W]hile more young people are participating in education for longer, the curriculum and qualifications they are pursuing contain too much that is not essential and too little which stretches them to achieve standards matching the best in the world. (Department for Education, 2010, p. 17)

[S]econdary schools have narrowed their focus and steered pupils away from GCSE courses towards less suitable qualifications which are deemed to be worth more than a GCSE, take no more time to teach and are seen as easier to pass. It is important that we should recognise good quality vocational qualifications, but we must avoid perverse incentives for schools to offer lower quality qualifications. (Department for Education, 2010, p. 68)

Against that background, the secretary of state invited Professor Alison Wolf to carry out a review of 14–19 vocational qualifications. Published in 2011, the Wolf Report was clear that –

Conventional academic study encompasses only part of what the labour market values and demands: vocational education can offer different content, different skills, different forms of teaching. Good vocational programmes are, therefore, respected, valuable and an important part of our, and any other country's, educational provision. . . . [However] Pre-16, it is critical that young people not be tracked in irreversible ways. (p. 7)

The government accepted all of Professor Wolf's recommendations. One consequence was that qualifications would only count in Key Stage 4 performance tables if they met the following criteria:

- They had a proven track record – only qualifications that had been taught for at least two years with good levels of take-up among 14–16-year-olds would be included.

- They offered pupils progression into a broad range of qualifications post-16 rather than a limited number in one or two occupational areas.

- They were at least the size of a GCSE.

- They had a substantial proportion of external assessment; and

- They had grades such as A*–G: qualifications with simple pass or fail results would be excluded. (Summarized from Department for Education, 2011d)

In addition, no qualification would be deemed equivalent to more than one GCSE.

Where next?

Delivering the inaugural Edge Foundation lecture in 2010, Michael Gove said:

> At crucial moments in the development of our education system the opportunity to embed high-quality technical routes for students was missed.
>
> As [the historian] Corelli Barnett has persuasively argued, the prevailing intellectual orthodoxy at the time of educational expansion in the late nineteenth and early twentieth century was disdainful of the practical and technical. While our competitors were ensuring that engineers, technicians and craftsmen were educated to the highest level, British – and specifically English – education reflected an inherited aristocratic disdain for trade. The highest goal of education was the preparation of young men for imperial administration, not the generation of innovation.

Setting out his vision of the future, he said:

> If one looks at those countries around the world that have the best technical education systems, core academic subjects are taught and assessed alongside – not in place of – technical learning until students reach 15 or 16.

That's why I floated the idea of an English Baccalaureate – a new certificate for all children who achieve a good GCSE pass in English, maths, a science, a modern or ancient language and a humanity like history or geography. But it's crucial to note that securing this core base of knowledge would not preclude the study of technical or vocational subjects.

It's not either/or but both/and.

This suggests a commitment to a broad and balanced school curriculum in which technical and vocational subjects may be taught side-by-side with academic subjects. Supporters of secondary technical education have also taken heart from the coalition government's support for a new network of high-quality UTCs – described earlier in this book by Kenneth Baker – and from a rapid expansion in the Apprenticeships programme.

On the other hand, a great deal of rhetoric points in the opposite direction. On 31 January 2012, the government published a list of the VRQs which would count in the 2014 Key Stage 4 performance tables: the press statement was headed 'Equivalent qualifications to be slashed from more than 3,175 to just 125' (Department for Education Press Release, www.education.gov.uk/inthenews/inthenews/a00202885/performancejan12). Press reports used terms like 'Mickey Mouse' and 'dead end' qualifications: there was barely any mention of those high-quality technical and vocational qualifications which will continue to count in school performance tables.

The success of the EBac seems, too, to point towards a revival of the academic traditions of Thomas Arnold and Robert Morant. In 2010, 22 per cent of Key Stage 4 students were entered for a full complement of EBac subjects. A survey carried out for the Department for Education showed that from September 2011, the proportion of students following a full set of EBac subjects had risen to 33 per cent among Year 11 students and 47 per cent among Year 10 students. At the same time, just under half of the schools in the survey (45%) said that a course or subject had been withdrawn from the curriculum or had failed to recruit enough students for the 2011–12 academic year. Most of these were VRQs, particularly BTECs (Clemens, 2011).

It was against this background that the leader of the Labour Party, Ed Miliband, proposed in October 2012 that a new Technical Baccalaureate should be introduced as a way of raising the profile and standing of vocational pathways for young people aged 14–18.

It seems that the debate, started so many decades ago, is not over.

Acknowledgement

I am immensely grateful to David Gillard for making so many key texts easily available online. His website, www.educationengland.org.uk, is a treasure trove!

APPENDIX 2
THE HISTORY AND STRENGTHS OF ENGLISH MIDDLE SCHOOLS

Nigel Wyatt

There are two stories to tell about the middle school system in England.

The first is about adapting resources to the growth and subsequent decline in pupil numbers. Explosive growth in pupil numbers between 1970 and 1982 led to the opening of over 1,800 middle schools in England, as local authorities sought efficient ways to introduce comprehensive education, cope with the raising of the school leaving age to 16 and cater for a steep rise in pupil numbers. The year 1982 was to be the high watermark, as middle schools began to close or were reorganized when pupil numbers began to fall again. This first story, then, is about the economics of catering for a large growth in pupil numbers at a time of rapid change and limited resources.

The second story, however, is about an attempt to provide a different model of education, one which sought to address some deep-seated reservations about the education system – a model tailored to the needs of children rather than the product of historical accident.

The fact that most children change schools at the age of 11 is largely a result of historical accident, rather than a deliberate choice. Sir Alec Clegg, for many years chief education officer of the West Riding of Yorkshire County Council. believed that dividing a child's educational journey into three stages, each of about four or five years, would enable schools to focus more clearly on the distinctive needs of children at each stage. In his vision, first schools would focus on the early years of a child's education. Middle schools would extend the best elements of primary education – particularly pastoral care and a powerful appreciation of the child as an individual – into Years 7 and 8 (age 11–13), while at the same time giving younger pupils access to more specialist teaching from the age of 9. Upper schools would cater for children from age 13 onwards: they would be a more adult institution, helping students prepare for public examinations. In the words of David Crook:

> Clegg's vision for middle schools went far beyond utilitarianism. He saw middle schools as places of hope, where strong pupil-teacher bonds would last beyond the traditional primary years, where pupils could experience teachers of specialist subjects earlier than in the secondary phase, and where pupils could be best supported as they experienced early adolescence. (2008, p. 17)

Part of the remit of the Plowden Committee in 1968 was to consider whether this was in fact the best arrangement. They, too, concluded that dividing the child's educational journey into three stages of about four or five years each would enable schools to focus more clearly on the distinctive needs of children at each stage (Department of Education and Science, 1967).

These educational arguments were largely neglected as local authorities started to close middle schools from the 1980s onwards. However, if we are to renew our vision of education in England, they deserve to be re-examined.

Middle schools – a system designed to meet the needs of young adolescents

Between the ages of 9 and 14, young people grow and change physically, intellectually, emotionally and socially at a rate greater than at any other time in their lives, except from birth to age 3. These years encompass the transition from the world of the young child to that of the young adult. It is distinctive of this time in their development that pupils work out for themselves who they are and what they believe.

Changing schools at age 11 means moving to a large institution, with a markedly different culture and ethos, and mingling with young people who are taller, larger, louder – and potentially very influential – just as they are in the midst of this increasing uncertainty and change.

There has been general concern about the pressures on young adolescents in modern society for some time. In 2007, the Secretary of State for Children, Schools and Families, Ed Balls, said in press interviews that children aged 8 to 13 – a group he called 'tweenagers' – were increasingly likely to experiment with alcohol, cigarettes and drugs. He was reported as saying that the transition from primary to secondary school was part of the problem because it meant moving from a small, supportive community to a larger, less personal environment (see, for example, BBC, 2007).

Concern for the healthy growth and development of young adolescents was also expressed in the Bailey Review *Letting Children Be Children*:

> Nearly nine out of 10 parents surveyed for this Review agreed with the statement that 'these days children are under pressure to grow up too quickly' (TNS Omnibus survey, 2011). This confirms what many parents, politicians, academics and commentators have suspected for some time, that this is a widely held concern of parents that needs to be taken seriously. (2011, p. 6)

Parents who participated in community events organized by the Cambridge Primary Review also shared these concerns – and clearly looked positively on the provision that middle schools make for children in this age group:

> Interestingly, parents in a number of other soundings commended a return to the middle school system to reduce the trauma of primary–secondary transfer and segregate younger children from the influence of teenagers. Contemporary anxieties are in this case prompting a desire to reinstate a pattern of schooling with which

an earlier generation had decided to dispense. (Alexander and Hargreaves, 2007, p. 39)

The Cambridge Primary Review research also suggests that middle school systems 'avoided the developmental double whammy of school transfer coinciding with the onset of puberty' (Alexander and Hargreaves, 2007, p. 38).

This is a central argument in favour of the middle school. Young people are provided with a relatively small and secure environment in which to thrive and develop. They learn with a group of staff who can specialize in teaching this age group and who know them well. This enables their intellectual and emotional needs to be met well within secure and clearly defined boundaries.

The distorting effect of assessment at age 11 and the narrowing of the curriculum in many schools – particularly at upper primary

National Curriculum assessments, colloquially known as SATs, loom large in the life of every primary school.

The original aim of SATs was to monitor each child's progress through Key Stages 1 to 3, with GCSEs and equivalent qualifications acting as a measure of their achievement at 16. In practice, SATs – especially at the end of Key Stage 2 – rapidly became the main measure of schools' own overall performance. In primary schools, SATs have a very powerful influence on what, how and when children are taught in Year 6 (age 10–11).

There has been growing unease about this. In 2008, for example, the House of Commons Children, Schools and Families Committee said:

We find that 'teaching to the test' and narrowing of the taught curriculum are widespread phenomena in schools, resulting in a disproportionate focus on the 'core' subjects of English, mathematics and science and, in particular, on those aspects of these subjects which are likely to be tested in an examination. Tests, however, can only test a limited range of the skills and activities which are properly part of a rounded education, so that a focus on improving test results compromises teachers' creativity in the classroom and children's access to a balanced curriculum. (p. 3)

In the same year, Ofsted's Chief Inspector Christine Gilbert wrote:

Survey inspections found that in some schools, overemphasising preparation for the national tests in English, mathematics and science, especially in Year 6, restricts the time available for activities that can most interest and challenge pupils: speaking and listening in English, using and applying mathematics, and scientific investigation. Pupils' attainment can then become narrowly based. More generally, focusing too much on the three core subjects can have negative effects on the curriculum in terms of breadth, balance and pupils' enjoyment. (Ofsted, 2008, p. 27)

Key Stage 2 SATs are not viewed in the same way in middle schools. Here, they are simply an indicator of progress made by children between Years 5 and 8, not the final measure of achievement during their whole time at the school. To judge a middle school's effectiveness by results produced only halfway through children's time there would be like judging the quality of cake when it has been mixed but not baked. Instead, middle schools use assessment formatively – that is, to inform the future development of the child.

A second issue with Key Stage 2 SATs is that they take place in the spring term of Year 6. Once they have taken their SATs, primary pupils' sights are firmly set on the autumn term and the start of a new life at secondary school. What happens in the summer term is neither here nor there.

Middle schools, on the other hand, are able to make productive use of the summer term by starting on Key Stage 3 courses – one of the factors evident when looking at progress made between Years 5 and 8. This has enabled middle schools to retain a more balanced curriculum for Years 5 and 6.

Specialist teaching in upper Key Stage 2

In evidence that echoes recommendations made in the 'Three Wise Men' report of 1992 (Alexander et al., 1992), the Cambridge Primary Review commented:

> [T]he generalist class teacher system is a legacy of the Victorian age when classes were huge, the curriculum was basic, and teachers were there to drill children in facts and skills. Its great strength was not educational, but financial – it was cheap. But schools have moved on in the past 150 years. (Cambridge Primary Review, 2009, p. 36)

Middle schools vary in their organization, but typically they will seek to create a smooth transition from the generalist world of the primary teacher to the subject specialist in a typical secondary school. Pupils benefit from specialist teaching in subjects such as modern foreign languages, technology and physical education. Middle schools are also equipped with specialist rooms and facilities, such as science labs. The experience of middle school staff is that pupils aged 9 and 10 thrive within this environment.

Managing the Key Stage 3 'dip'

There is evidence that pupil performance can plateau or fall in the year or two following transfer from one school to another. The phenomenon has been widely identified not only in England, but in many countries. In a study of 14 countries, dips were suggested in 9; only 1 country stated that dips did not occur (Whitby and Lord, 2006, p. 2).

It is commonly asserted that in three-tier (or middle school) systems pupils are doubly disadvantaged because there are two points of transfer, most commonly at 9 and again at 13. However, there is a lack of hard evidence to support these assertions. On the contrary, Maurice Galton, a leading British researcher in this field, said, 'the evidence supports the view that delaying the move from the elementary school helps to reduce dips in transfer.' He went on to say that 'There is less of a case for arguing that the dips are cumulative so that pupils attending a three-tier system of schooling are permanently disadvantaged' (2006, p. 45).

A year later, a small-scale study used data from QCA Optional Tests to explore the Key Stage 3 'dip'. This study also found that pupils in middle schools were less likely to see a dip in their performance in Years 7 and 8 than pupils in secondary schools (Pepper, 2007, p. 31).

What all this means for individual children entering Key Stage 3 in the two forms of schooling is interestingly revealed in an illuminative small-scale study by Dr Jenny Symonds. She interviewed and surveyed two matched groups of children from primary and middle school as they moved to Key Stage 3. The research identified first that the two most powerful factors influencing children's attitude and perception of school were relationships with teachers and enjoyment of lessons. Interviews revealed marked differences between the two types of school in the experience of the pupils. In middle school, the pupils generally worked with about 9 teachers who knew them well. The pupils spoke warmly of the schools' social environment and the good quality of teacher–pupil relationships. In contrast the pupils in secondary school encountered about 20 different teachers and reported difficulties in managing their different expectations. None of the secondary school pupils interviewed reported having a personal relationship with their teachers and were perceptive in reporting that teachers often seemed more concerned with managing pupil behaviour.

> The findings suggest that it is easier for better quality teacher-pupil relationships to develop in middle schools given that children encounter less teachers and have prior opportunity to get to know them well. Middle schools, in their form of organisation and curriculum provision, need to ensure that they can provide the best circumstances for these relationships to develop . . .
>
> Stationing school transition in early adolescence appears to make children feel more grown up, and for some this influences the amount of autonomy they want at school. Unfortunately the children in this study did not find that their new school granted them more autonomy.

Instead, they perceived their teachers as strict and controlling and soon began to form impressions of their teachers as impersonal adults. (Symonds, 2010)

The children's perceptions of school both showed some decline during Years 7 and 8. However, middle school children started Year 7 with more positive feelings about their schooling, and these feelings diminished much more slowly.

Conclusion

Middle schools – in the past, a neglected part of the English educational landscape – offer both an interesting model for the future of education in England and a great deal of valuable experience. They provide a safe, nurturing environment for the young adolescent, while offering a broad, varied curriculum and early access to specialist teachers and facilities. There is also evidence that they may lessen some of the effects of regression on transfer at 11 and the dip in progress during Key Stage 3.

GLOSSARY

Berufsbildende Höhere Schule vocational high school (Austria)
Berufsbildende Mittlere Schule secondary vocational school (Austria)
Black Country UTC Black Country UTC is a school in England which opened in 2011 to give 14–18-year-olds with an interest in science and engineering the chance to learn and succeed in an inspirational institution, using the latest technology that industry has to offer and supported by expert staff. The aim of the Black Country curriculum is to give students insights into the very wide range of careers open to people with high-level knowledge and skills in science and engineering.
BRIT School The BRIT School, a specialist performing arts and technology school, is sponsored by the British Record Industry Trust. The BRIT School is an independent, state-funded City College for the Technology of the Arts, the first of its kind in England to be dedicated to education and vocational training for the performing arts, media, art and design and the technologies that make performance possible.
Career Academy Programs These US programs typically enrol young people in Grade 9 (age 14) and carry them through high school graduation (age 17).
Career and Technical Education (CTE) In the past two decades new models of vocational education have emerged in the United States that demonstrate that it is possible to combine rigorous academic studies with career training in high-skill, high-demand fields. In order to differentiate these kinds of programmes from vocational education in the more traditional trades, the term Career and Technical Education has come into use. These models are best

seen in a set of national programmes that have acquired sufficient scale to become important players in the high school reform world.

Career and Technical High Schools These schools have been introduced in the past five years in certain American cities. These start at 14 and continue on to 18 and 19.

Dual Credit Programme An option for students in Ontario who want to earn high school credits while studying at a local college or taking apprenticeship training. This bears similarities to the dual system in Austria.

General Certificate of Secondary Education (GCSE) The GCSE is an academic qualification awarded in a specified subject, generally taken in a number of subjects by students aged 14–16 in secondary education in England, Wales and Northern Ireland and is equivalent to a Level 2 (A*–C) and Level 1 (D–G) in the Qualifications and Curriculum Framework.

High Schools That Work (HSTW) HSTW is a network of schools in the United States, including over 1,200 schools, mostly in the south where many high schools continue to have a strong vocational track. The focus of HSTW has been to ensure that students in a vocational track are getting a rigorous academic education, especially in mathematics and science, albeit typically taught in a more applied fashion.

Höhere Technische Lehranstalten higher technical institute (Austria)

Key Stage The Key Stages were first defined in the 1988 Education Reform Act to accompany the introduction of the National Curriculum in England, Wales and Northern Ireland. The precise definition of each of the main 4 Key Stages is age related, incorporating all pupils of a particular age at the beginning of each academic year.

Linked Learning With funding from the James Irvine Foundation, Linked Learning is developing career academies in such major California industry sectors as building and environmental design, biomedical and health sciences and arts, media and entertainment. Each academy is designed in such a way as to meet the academic course-taking requirements for admission to California's four-year universities as well as providing advanced technical preparation in a career area.

Middle Schools These English schools offer the opportunity for children aged between 8 and 12 or 9 and 13 to flourish and grow in a comparatively small and secure environment before making the choices which will affect the rest of their lives; they offer the chance for children to experience a broad and balanced curriculum in a climate free from the crushing oppression of GCSEs.

National Academy Foundation (NAF) NAF academies (USA) mainly prepare young people in four career areas – finance, engineering, ICT and hospitality and tourism – with health care set to become the fifth specialist field. A key feature of the NAF design is that all students are provided with a 6–10 week paid internship by one of 2,500 corporate partners.

National Curriculum This was introduced into England, Wales and Northern Ireland as a nationwide curriculum for primary and secondary state schools following the Education Reform Act of 1988.

Oxford Cambridge and RSA Examinations (OCR) This is a UK awarding body which provides qualifications for learners of all ages at school, college, in work or through part-time learning programmes.

Programme for International Student Assessment (PISA) PISA tests assess the reading, maths and science skills of young people at the age of about 14. They do not provide a comprehensive overview of the successes and failures of any single education system. PISA tests are administered by the OECD.

Samuel Whitbread Academy This is a high school in Bedfordshire, England. Formerly a community college, it is a high school – or upper school – in a three-tier system, taking students from three middle schools at the age of 13.

Specialist High Skills Majors The SHSM provides a menu of options for students in Ontario, including those who are unenthusiastic about a purely academic curriculum.

Studio Schools These are 14–18 schools in England. They generally support around 300 students. With year-round opening and a 9–5 working day, they feel more like a workplace than a school. Working closely with local employers, Studio Schools offer a range of academic and vocational qualifications including GCSEs in English, maths and science, as well as paid work placements linked directly to employment opportunities in the local area.

Universities and Colleges Admissions Service (UCAS) UCAS is the British admission service for students applying to university and college.

Young Apprenticeship (YA) This was developed to offer motivated 14–16-year-old pupils the opportunity to take industry-specific vocational qualifications alongside their programme of GCSEs. The pupils spent three days in school, one day at an FE college and one day in a workplace.

REFERENCES

Alexander, R. and Hargreaves, L. (2007), *Community Soundings: The Primary Review Regional Witness Sessions*. Cambridge: University of Cambridge.

Alexander, R., Rose, J. and Woodhead, C. (1992), *Curriculum Organisation and Classroom Practice in Primary Schools: A Discussion Paper*. London: Department of Education and Science.

Audit Commission for Local Authorities and the National Health Service in England and Wales (1990), *Rationalising Primary School Provision*. London: HMSO.

Bailey, B. (1990), 'Technical education and secondary schooling 1905–1945', in P. Summerfield and E. Evans (eds), *Technical Education and the State since 1850*. Manchester: Manchester University Press.

Bailey, R. (2011), *Letting Children Be Children: Report of an Independent Review of the Commercialisation and Sexualisation of Childhood*, Cm 8078. Norwich: Stationery Office.

Barber, M. (2007), *Instruction to Deliver*. London: Politico's.

BBC (2007), '*Tweenagers' Need More Support*, BBC News website, 19 November 2007. Available at http://news.bbc.co.uk/1/hi/education/7102210.stm [Accessed 30 August 2012].

Board of Education (1927), *Report of the Consultative Committee on the Education of the Adolescent* (Hadow Report). London: HMSO.

— (1938), *Report of the Consultative Committee on Secondary Education, with Special Reference to Grammar Schools and Technical High Schools* (Spens Report). London: HMSO.

— (1943), *Curriculum and Examinations in Secondary Schools: Report of the Committee of the Secondary School Examinations Council* (Norwood Report). London: HMSO.

Callaghan, J. (1976), Speech at Ruskin College Oxford. Available at www.educationengland.org.uk/documents/speeches/1976ruskin.html [Accessed 23 July 2012].

Cambridge Primary Review (2009), *Introducing the Cambridge Primary Review*. Available at www.primaryreview.org.uk/downloads/CPR_revised_booklet.pdf [Accessed 2 August 2012].

Carneville, A. P., Smith, N. and Strohl, J. (2010), *Help Wanted: Projections of Jobs and Education Requirements Through 2018*. Georgetown: Georgetown University Center on Education and the Workforce.

CBI (Confederation of British Industry) (2010), *Ready to Grow: Business Priorities for Education and Skills*. London: CBI.

— (2011), *Building for Growth: Education and Skills Survey 2011*. London: CBI.

Clemens, S. (2011), *The English Baccalaureate and GCSE Choices*. Research Brief RB 150. London: Department for Education.

Crawford, M. (2009), *The Case for Working with Your Hands: Or Why Office Work Is Bad for Us and Fixing Things Feels Good*. London: Viking Penguin.

Crook, D. (2008), *'The Middle School Cometh' . . . and Goeth: Alec Clegg and the Rise and Fall of the English Middle School*. Available at http://eprints. ioe.ac.uk/4661/1/Crook2008Themiddleschool117.pdf [Accessed 25 July 2012].

Department for Business, Innovation and Skills (2011), *Higher Education: Students at the Heart of the System*, Cm 8122. Norwich: Stationery Office.

Department for Education (2010), *The Importance of Teaching*, Cm 7980. Norwich: Stationery Office.

— (2011a), *Statistical Release: National Pupil Projections* (OSR 12/2011). Available at www.education.gov.uk/rsgateway/DB/STR/d001017/osr12– 2011v2.pdf [Accessed 20 July 2012].

— (2011b), *The Framework for the National Curriculum: A Report by the Expert Panel for the National Curriculum Review*. London: Department for Education.

— (2011c), *Wolf Review of Vocational Education: Government Response*. London: Department for Education.

— (2011d), *Qualifications for 14–16 Year Olds and Performance Tables: Technical Guidance for Awarding Organisations*. Available at http://media. education.gov.uk/assets/files/pdf/c/consultation%20response%20on%20 qualifications%20for%2014–16-year-olds%20and%20performance%20 tables.pdf [Accessed 23 July 2012].

— (2011e), *Remit for Review of the National Curriculum in England*. Available at https://www.education.gov.uk/schools/teachingandlearning/curriculum/ nationalcurriculum/b0073043/remit-for-review-of-the-national-curriculum-in -england [Accessed 24 July 2012].

— (2012), *Statistical Release: NEET Statistics Quarterly Brief Quarter 1 2012*. Available at www.education.gov.uk/rsgateway/DB/STR/d001064/osr09– 2012.pdf [Accessed 20 July 2012].

Department for Education Press Release (7 December 2010), *Secretary of State comments on PISA study of school systems*. Available at www.education.gov.uk/inthenews/inthenews/a0070008/secretary-of- state-comments-on-pisa-study-of-school-systems [Accessed 24 July 2012].

Department for Education and Employment (2001), *Schools: Building on Success*, Cmnd 5050. London: HMSO.

Department for Education and Skills (2001), *Schools: Achieving Success*, Cm 5230. London: HMSO.

— (2004), *14–19 Curriculum and Qualifications Reform: Final Report of the Working Group on 14–19 Reform* (Tomlinson Report). Annesley: Department for Education and Science Publications.

— (2005), *14–19 Education and Skills*, Cm 6476. Norwich: HMSO.

— (1965), *Circular 10/65: The Organisation of Secondary Education*. London: HMSO.

— (1967), *Children and Their Primary Schools: A Report of the Central Advisory Council for Education (England)* (Plowden Report). London: HMSO.

Department of Education and Science and Welsh Office (1981), *The School Curriculum*. London: HMSO.

Department for Education Statistical First Release 15/2011 (2011), *Participation in Education, Training and Employment by 16–18 Year Olds in England*. Available at www.education.gov.uk/rsgateway/DB/SFR/s001011/sfr15–2011.pdf [Accessed 1 October 2012].

Department for Education Statistical First Release 01/2012 (2012), *GCE/Applied GCE A/AS and Equivalent Examination Results in England, 2010/11*. Available at www.media.education.gov.uk/assets/files/pdf/s/sfr01–2012.pdf [Accessed 1 October 2012].

Department for Education Statistical First Release 03/2012 (2012), *GCSE and Equivalent Attainment by Pupil Characteristics in England, 2010/11*. Available from www.education.gov.uk/rsgateway/DB/SFR/s001057/sfr03–2012.pdf [Accessed 2 October 2012].

Department for Work and Pensions and Department for Education (2011), *A New Approach to Child Poverty: Tackling the Causes of Disadvantage and Transforming Families Lives*, Cm 8061. Norwich: Stationery Office.

Education Quality and Accountability Office (2010), *Programme for International Student Assessment (PISA), 2009 Highlights of Ontario Student Results*. Available at www.eqao.com/pdf_e/10/2009_PISA_Highlights_en.pdf [Accessed 24 July 2012].

Edwards, R. (1960), *The Secondary Technical School*. London: University of London Press.

European Union (2012), *European Economic Forecast, Spring 2012*. Available at http://ec.europa.eu/economy_finance/publications/european_economy/2012/pdf/ee-2012–1_en.pdf [Accessed 28 August 2012].

Eurostat (2012), *Young People Aged 18–24 Not in Employment and Not in Any Education and Training, by Sex and NUTS 1 Regions (NEET rates)*, updated 6 August 2012. Available at http://appsso.eurostat.ec.europa.eu/nui/show.do?dataset=edat_lfse_22&lang=en [Accessed 28 August 2012].

Federal Chancellery (2011), 'Education at a glance 2011', in *News from Austria*. Available at www.bka.gv.at/site/infodate__26.09.2011/7459/default.aspx#id44956 [Accessed 24 July 2012].

Federal Ministry for Education, Arts and Culture (2009), 'New middle school', in *Austrian Education News*, issue 60. Available at www.bmukk.gv.at/medienpool/18886/aen_09_04_60.pdf [Accessed 24 July 2012].

— (2011), 'Working in training firms', in *Austrian Education News*, issue 65. Available at www.bmukk.gv.at/medienpool/20247/aen_65.pdf [Accessed 24 July 2012].

Flew, A. (1987), *Power to the Parents: Reversing Educational Decline*. London: Sherwood.

Frosh, S., Phoenix, A. and Pattman, R. (2003), 'The trouble with boys', in *The Psychologist*, 16, 84–7.

Galton, M. (2006), 'Are dips in attainment at transfer cumulative? in Suffolk County Council', *School Organisation Review: Pupil Performance Research Findings Part 2*. Available at www.suffolk.gov.uk/assets/suffolk.gov.uk/Education%20and%20Careers/Children%20and%20Young%20People/Schools%20&%20Support%20in%20Education/School%20Organisation%20Review%20(SOR)/Background%20and%20Archive/Policy%20Development%20Panel%20Report%20Annex%205.pdf [Accessed 25 July 2012].

Gillard, D. (2011), *Education in England: A Brief History*. Available online at www.educationengland.org.uk/history [Accessed 23 July 2012].

Gove, M. (2010), Speech to the Edge Foundation. Available at www.education.gov.uk/inthenews/speeches/a0064364/michael-gove-to-the-edge-foundation [Accessed 23 July 2012].

Government of Ontario (2011), *81 Per Cent of High School Students Graduating*. Available online at http://news.ontario.ca/opo/en/2011/03/81-per-cent-of-high-school-students-graduating.html [Accessed 24 July 2012].

Hadrill, W. P. (1955), 'Vocational and near-vocational interests in the curriculum of the secondary modern school', in *Journal of Vocational Education & Training*, 7, 14, 45–58.

Halperin, S. (ed.) (1988), *The Forgotten Half: Non-College-Bound Youth in America*. Washington, DC: William T. Grant Foundation.

Hoeckel, K. (2010), *Learning for Jobs: OECD Reviews of Vocational Education and Training – Austria*. Paris: OECD Publications. Available at www.oecd.org/dataoecd/29/33/45407970.pdf [Accessed 24 July 2012].

House of Commons (1884), *Report of the Royal Commission on Technical Instruction* (Samuelson Report), HC 1884.

House of Commons Children, Schools and Families Committee (2008), *Third Report of Session 2007–08: Testing and Assessment* (HC169–1). London: Stationery Office.

House of Commons Education Committee (2011), *Fifth Report of Session 2010–12: The English Baccalaureate, Volume 1* (HC851). London: Stationery Office.

Joint Council for Qualifications (JCQ) (2010), *Provisional GCSE (Full Course) Results – June 2010*. Available at www.jcq.org.uk/attachments/

published/1317/JCQ%20Results%2024–08–10.pdf [Accessed 1 October 2012].

— (2011), *Provisional GCSE (Full Course) Results – June 2011.* Available at www.jcq.org.uk/attachments/published/1589/GCSE%20RESULTS.pdf [Accessed 19 July 2012].

Medhat, S. (2009), *A Shortage of Technicians*. London: New Engineering Foundation.

Migration Watch (12 August 2010), *Immigration and Unemployment.* Available at www.migrationwatchuk.org/briefingPaper/document/199 [Accessed 20 July 2012].

Ministry of Education (1959), *15 to 18: A Report of the Central Advisory Council for Education (England)* (Crowther Report). London: HMSO.

— (1963), *Half Our Future: A Report of the Central Advisory Council for Education (England)* (Newsom Report). London: HMSO.

Musgrove, F. (1964), *Youth and the Social Order*. London: Routledge and Kegan Paul.

National Foundation for Educational Research (2011), *Review of the National Curriculum in England: Report on Subject Breadth in International Jurisdictions*. Research Report DFE-RR178a. London: Department for Education.

Oates, T. (2010), *Could Do Better: Using International Comparisons to Refine the National Curriculum in England*. Cambridge: Cambridge Assessment. Available at www.cambridgeassessment.org.uk/ca/digitalAssets/188853_Could_do_better_FINAL_inc_foreword.pdf [Accessed 24 July 2012].

OECD (2009), *Education at a Glance 2009*. Paris: OECD Publishing.

— (2010a), *Learning for Jobs*. Paris: OECD Publishing.

— (2010b), *Off to a Good Start? Jobs for Youth*. Paris: OECD Publishing.

— (2010c), *Strong Performers and Successful Reformers in Education: Lessons from PISA for the United States*. Paris: OECD Publications. Available from www.oecd.org/dataoecd/32/50/46623978.pdf [Accessed 24 July 2012].

— (2011a), *Economic Surveys: Austria*. Paris: OECD Publishing.

— (2011b), *Economic Surveys: Austria*. Available at www.oecd.org/dataoecd/53/47/48306099.pdf [Accessed 24 July 2012].

ONS (Office for National Statistics) (13 July 2011), *Statistical Bulletin: Labour Market Statistics*. Available at www.ons.gov.uk/ons/rel/lms/labour-market-statistics/lms-july-2011/index.html [Accessed 20 July 2012].

Ofsted (2008), *The Annual Report of Her Majesty's Chief Inspector of Education, Children's Services and Skills 2007/08*. London: Stationery Office.

Ontario Ministry of Education (2010), *What Do You Need to Graduate?* Available online at www.edu.gov.on.ca/extra/eng/ppm/graduate.html [Accessed 24 July 2012].

Ontario Ministry of Education (2011), *Specialist High Skills Majors*. Available online at www.edu.gov.on.ca/eng/studentsuccess/pathways/shsm/shsm_fact_sheet.pdf [Accessed 24 July 20120].

Pepper, D. (2007), *The Key Stage 3 Dip: Myth or Reality?* Available at www. scribd.com/doc/6367591/The-Key-Stage-3-dip-myth-or-reality [Accessed 25 July 2012].

Prais, S., Halsey, H., Postlethwaite, N,. Smithers, A. and Steedman, H. (1991), *Every Child in Britain: Report of the Channel Four Commission*. London: Broadcasting Support Services.

Pring, R., Hayward, G., Hodgson, A., Johnson, J., Keep, E., Oancea, A., Rees, G., Spours, K. and Wilde, S. (2009), *Education for All: The Future of Education and Training for 14–19 Year Olds*. Abingdon: Routledge.

Ramsden, S., Richardson, F., Josse, G., Thomas, M., Ellis, C., Shakeshaft, C., Seghier, M. and Price, C. (2011), 'Verbal and non-verbal intelligence changes in the teenage brain', *Nature* 479 (3 November), 113–16.

Richardson, W. and Sing, S. (2011), *The Impact of Practical and 'Vocational' Learning on Academically-Able Young People Aged 11–16*. London: Edge Foundation.

Richardson, W. and Wiborg, S. (2010), *English Technical and Vocational Education in Historical and Comparative Perspective*. London: Edge Foundation and Baker Dearing Educational Trust.

Russell Group (2011), *Informed Choices: A Russell Group Guide to Making Decisions About Post-16 Education*. Available at http://russellgroup.org/ Informed%20Choices%20final.pdf [Accessed 20 July 2012].

Smithers, A. and Robinson, P. (1991), *Beyond Compulsory Schooling*. London: Council for Industry and Higher Education.

— (2009), *Specialist Science Schools*. Buckingham: Carmichael Press.

— (2010), *Choice and Selection in School Admissions: The Experience of Other Countries*. Buckingham: Carmichael Press.

— (2011), *Gifted and Talented Education in English Schools.* London: Sutton Trust.

Sternberg, R. J. (2011), 'The theory of successful intelligence', in R. J. Sternberg and S. B. Kaufman (eds), *The Cambridge Handbook of Intelligence*. New York: Cambridge University Press.

Strachey, L. (1918), *Eminent Victorians*. Project Gutenberg EBook, www. gutenberg.org/cache/epub/2447/pg2447.txt [Accessed 23 July 2012].

Symonds, J. E. (2010), *Are UK Middle Schools Better for Early Adolescents than Transition into Secondary School? A Study of Two School Environments*. [Word] Available at www.middleschools.org.uk/documents/ research/J%20Symonds%20-%20Comparing%20two%20school%20 environments%20-%202010.docx [Accessed 2 August 2012].

Symonds, W. C., Schwartz, R. B. and Ferguson, R. (2011), *Pathways to Prosperity: Meeting the Challenge of Preparing Young Americans for the 21st Century*. Report issued by the Pathways to Prosperity Project. Harvard: Harvard School of Education.

TES (Times Educational Supplement) (16 February 2001), *Are You a Bog-Standard Secondary?* Available at www.tes.co.uk/article. aspx?storycode=343807 [Accessed 20 July 2012].

Vlaeminke, M. (1990), 'The subordination of technical education in secondary schooling, 1870–1914', in P. Summerfield and E. Evans (eds), *Technical Education and the State since 1850*. Manchester: Manchester University Press.

West, J. and Steedman, H. (2003), *Finding Our Way: Vocational Education in England*. London: Centre for Economic Performance, London School of Economics.

Whitby, K. and Lord, P. (2006), *Dips in Performance and Motivation: A Purely English Perception?* Slough: National Foundation for Educational Research.

Wolf, A. (2011), *Review of Vocational Education* (Wolf Report). London: Department for Education.

Young, D. (1990), *The Enterprise Years*. London: Headline Book Publishing.

INDEX

Advanced Supplementary (AS)
    qualification 47
aerospace and aircraft maintenance 66
American perspective of pathways
    and European employers, cultural
        differences 79
    extracurricular activities 78
    Finland schools 78
    high school and HE dropout
        data 72
    implications 82–4
        build-on-what-works strategy 83
        mix of classroom and
            workplace-based learning 83–4
        university preparation for
            courses 83
        university sponsorship 83
        work-based learning 83
    'Learning for Jobs' 72
    'middle skill' jobs 72
    new career and technical
        education 74–7
        aligned academic course work 76
        'at-risk' students 76
        career academy programs 75
        common elements 76
        Germany/Switzerland/
            Denmark 77
        highquality upper secondary
            vocational system 77

High Schools That Work
    (HSTW) 75
    NAF academies 75
    Project Lead the Way 75
'Off to a Good Start? Jobs for
    Youth' 72
options of organizing 79–82
    Linked Learning 80–1
    lower and upper secondary
        education, distinction
        between 81
    universalize career academy
        model 79–80
    university pathway,
        career-focused 80–1
principles 78
vocational education
    in comprehensive high
        schools 73
    rise of the standards
        movement 74
apprenticeship
    'dual system' of 21, 110
    European-style 79
    Young Apprenticeship (YA) 38
arts college, sports/creative 35–8
    BRIT School (case study) 36–8
    specialisms 35–6
Austria
    academic secondary school 108

academic selection at age 10 108
compulsory education 107
general secondary school 108
middle schools 108–9
mixed-ability teaching 108
PISA tests 107
Secondary level 2
  Berufsschule – compulsory vocational schools 110
  cross-curricular teaching and group projects 110
  'dual system' of apprenticeship 110
  pre-vocational schools 110
  specialization 109
  technical or vocational pathway 109
success of technical and vocational education 110–11

baccalaureate structure 53–4
Berufsbildende Höhere Schule (vocational high school) 109
Berufsbildende Mittlere Schule (secondary vocational school) 109
Bill and Melinda Gates Foundation 79
Black Country UTC, Walsall 21, 30–2, 51
boarding schools 88
BRIT School 36–8

Career Academy Programs 75
Career and Technical Education (CTE) 40, 74–7
Career and Technical High Schools 40–1
career pathway: career college 21, 38–41
  American Career and technical high schools (case study) 40–1

Food and Finance High School, Manhattan 41
Studio School 39–40
Wolf Report on Vocational Education 39
Young Apprenticeships (YAs) 38
The Case for Working with Your Hands 12
Certificate of Extended Education (CEE) 46
Certificate of Pre-Vocational Education (CPVE) 46
Children and Their Primary Schools (1967 Plowden Report) 6
City and Guilds 365 46
college
  arts, sports/creative 35–8
  BRIT School (case study) 36–8
  career 38–41
  FE 23
  liberal arts 32–5
  sixth-form 57
  specialisms 35–6
  tertiary 57
  UTC 22, 27–32
Creative arts 20, 21, 35–8
14–19 Curriculum and Qualifications Reform, Tomlinson Report 2

diplomas, levels
  Entry, Foundation, Intermediate, Advanced 54
Dual Credit Programme 113
'dual system' of apprenticeship 21, 110

Early College High Schools (ECHS) 81–2
14–18 education
  adapting new pattern 68

Belgium 61
current assortment 57–8
  'Free' schools 58
  '14–18,' preferred 58
differentiation at age 14 65–7
  immigration 66
  National Qualifications
    Framework 66–7
  reason for different routes 65
  upper secondary education 66
differentiation in education 63–4
  education in other countries 64
  11+ examination 63
  gifted and talented pupils 63
  grammar school education 63
England de facto 62
Germany 61
good understanding of arithmetic 1
importance of learning by
    doing 10–12
  egalitarian theories of
    education 11–12
  grammar school 11
  left-handedness 11
  self-esteem 11
influence of exams at 7–10, 16
  assessment of pupil's progress 8
  BTECs and OCR Nationals 10
  English Baccalaureate
    (EBac), 10
  GCSEs 8–9
  Key Stage 4, 8
  VRQs 9
  Wolf Report on Vocational
    Education 8
intermediate schools in France and
    Japan 61
lessons from research 12–14
  abstract and analytical
    learning 14

impact of practical learning 13–14
  theory of 'successful
    intelligence' 12
lower secondary 62
Netherlands 61
New Zealand 61
Nordic pattern 61
OECD 61, 67
14–19 'phase' of education and
    training 1
routes from age 14, 64–5
secondary education in
    England 3–7
split at age 16
  'facilitating' subjects 59
  GCSEs at age 16, 58
  industry-specific/vocationally
    related qualifications 59
  lengthening compulsory
    education 60
  vocational education pre-16,
    objections 59–60
Studio Schools Trust 64
Sweden 61
training 62
Upper secondary education 62
UTCs 64
vocational route in Switzerland,
    Denmark and Germany 62
Working Group for 14–19
    Reform 2
Education Act (1944) 4, 27, 44, 93,
    126
Educational Reconstruction
    Committee of the Board of
    Education in 1940–1 4
*Education for All: The Future of
    Education and Training for
    14–19 Year Olds* 55
engineering 34, 66

at the Black Country UTC,
Walsall 21
career areas 75
civil 121
curriculum 31
electrical 109, 121
GCSE 8
German for 23, 29
mechanical 121
NAF's engineering academies 75
pre-engineering program 75
qualifications in 31
social 5
workshops 31
England de facto 62
England, education in
alternative vision
education in three phases 16
middle schools 17
Plowden Report 17–18
primary education 17
common entitlement 22–4
aims 22
Diplomas 23
employability skills or personal
learning and thinking skills 24
English and maths 23
further education (FE) college 23
current school year/Key Stage
structure 16
decision making at age of 14,
19–20
National Curriculum, review
of 15–16
panel's proposals 16
reconfiguring the school
estates 24–5
secondary education 18–19
Key Stage 4 (ages 14–16) 18
single phase of 14–18
education 19

14–18 years 20–2
career pathway 21
liberal arts pathway 21
pattern in UTC 22
sports and creative arts
pathway 21
technical pathway 21
English middle schools
assessment at age 11 and upper
primary 144–5
managing the Key Stage 3
'dip' 146–8
needs of young adolescents 142–4
specialist teaching in upper Key
Stage 2 146
extracurricular activities 78

Fine arts 35
*The Forgotten Half: Non-College
Bound Youth in America* 71
France 49, 61, 64, 134
'Free' schools 58
further education (FE) college 23, 29,
31, 38, 40, 46, 57, 64, 68, 71,
78, 116

Gates Foundation 79, 81
General Certificate of Secondary
Education (GCSE), 2–3, 7–10,
14, 31–2, 35, 38–40, 43,
46–52, 54–5, 58–9, 61, 67–8,
95, 102–3, 105, 111, 117,
134–9, 144
and A-levels
Ron Dearing's Review of
Qualifications for 16–19 year
olds (1996) 47
Tomlinson Report (2004) 47
General National Vocational
Qualifications (GNVQs) 46,
133, 134, 136

Germany 7, 21, 38, 40, 60–1, 64, 67, 73, 76–7, 83, 134

Gove, Michael (Secretary of State for Education) 10, 15, 44, 55, 105, 106, 136, 138

grammar school 4–5, 11, 27, 30, 57, 63, 86, 91–4, 119, 122–6

High Schools That Work (HSTW) 75

Höhere Technische Lehranstalten (higher technical institute) 109

independent school perspective
  boarding schools 88
  catch-up lessons or subject 'clinics' 94
  Education Act (1944) 93
  13+ entry point 87
  first year of senior school 88
  Girls' Day Schools' Trust, influence of 86
  grammar school 92
  'great public school tradition' 86
  King's College School, Wimbledon 85
  lower school 90
  modern grammar schools 93
  one-size-fits-all educational economy 93
  personal attention 94
  preparatory schools 86–8
  school areas of vocational education 95
  schools in the independent sector 90
  senior school 88–9
  transfer of boys at age of 13 86–7
  unemployment 95–6
  well-organized lower school model 91
  work ethos and skills of British youth 95

International Baccalaureate Career-Related Certificate (IBCC) 52

International Baccalaureate (IB) 47, 54

International GCSE (IGCSE) 47

James Irvine Foundation 80–1

Japan 49, 61, 66, 134

JCB Academy, Rocester 20, 28, 30

job shadowing 78

Key Stage 7–9, 15–16, 18, 34, 37, 50, 55, 59, 68–9, 98–9, 101–2, 133, 135–7, 139, 144–8

King's College School, Wimbledon 85, 86

learning programmes
  core learning 54
  main learning 54

liberal arts college 32–5
  'academic' curriculum 32
  Samuel Whitbread Academy (case study) 33–5
  University of Exeter research for the Edge Foundation 32

Linked Learning 80–1

medical science 66

mentoring 28, 78, 116

middle school(s) 6, 17
  Austria 108–9
  education 97–103
  English
    assessment at age 11 and upper primary 144–5
    managing the Key Stage 3 'dip' 146–8
    needs of young adolescents 142–4
    specialist teaching in upper Key Stage 2 146

perspective
    feeder lower schools 100
    literacy 101
    middle schools, opportunities
        in 99–100, 102–3
    National Curriculum 98
        Key Stages 99
    Parkfields Middle School in
        Toddington 100–1
    Post Graduate Certificate in
        Education (PGCE) 102
    ROSLA (Raising of School
        Leaving Age) 99
Modern grammar schools 93

nanotechnology 66
National Academy Foundation
    (NAF) 75–6, 80
    career academy 80
National Council for Vocational
    Education 46
National Curriculum 1, 2, 8, 9, 15,
    17, 18, 22, 37, 39, 40, 49–50,
    64, 98, 99, 106, 111, 115,
    131, 133, 144
    in England, review of 106
    Finnish classroom practice into the
        UK 106
National Institute for Economic and
    Social Research 59
National Qualifications
    Framework 66–7
National Vocational Qualifications
    (NVQs) 46
Netherlands 61, 64, 67, 76, 83
New Zealand 61
Nordic pattern 61
nuclear industry 66

one-size-fits-all 93
Ontario, Canada 111–14

compulsory credits 111–12
dual credit programme 113
education policy 111
elementary (age 6–14) and
    secondary (age 14–18) 111
optional credits 112–13
post-compulsory education 114
SHSMs 113
Ontario Secondary School
    Diploma 54, 111
Organisation of Economic and
    Cultural Development
    (OECD) 49, 61–2, 67, 72, 105,
    110, 111–14, 134
Oxford Cambridge and RSA
    Examinations (OCR) 8–10, 136
    Nationals 8–10, 136

Parkfields Middle School in
    Toddington 100–1
pathways
    American
        perspective see American
        perspective of pathways
    14–18 years
        career college 38–41
        liberal arts college 32–5
        sports and creative arts
            college 35–8
        university technical college
            27–32
Performing arts 25, 32, 35–7
personal attention 94
pharmaceuticals 66
Post Graduate Certificate in
    Education (PGCE) 102
post-war technical schools 125–6
Preparatory schools 86–8
Programme for International Student
    Assessment (PISA) 105–7,
    111, 113

countries performing well in PISA
tests 107
parental attitudes 107

qualifications
changes to current 51–6
apprenticeship route 53
assessment methods 52
of GCSEs and A-levels 51
literacy and numeracy knowledge
and skills 51
modular structures for
examinations 52
review and recalibrate the
standards 53
single awarding body 52–3
technical content of vocational
courses 52
diplomas at four levels
Entry, Foundation, Intermediate,
Advanced 54
'gold standard' A-levels. 55
Working Group's proposals 54
GCSEs and A-levels 47
International GCSE (IGCSE) 47
Ron Dearing's Review of
Qualifications for 16–19 year
olds (1996) 47
Tomlinson Report (2004) 47
GCSEs replacement by
assessment system 50
general qualifications 50
grade inflation 49
Graduation Certificate at 18+ 55–6
history 43–5
A-levels certificates 45
CSE 44
EBac 44
Education Act (1944) 44
'gold standard' qualification 45
Higher School Certificate 44

O-levels 44–5
post-16 curriculum 44
initiatives 43
Key Stage 4 55
learning programmes
core learning 54
main learning 54
mathematics and English up to age
of 18, recognition for 50
National Curriculum 50
teaching to the test 48
vocational qualifications 46
Wolf Report 46

recommendations 115–17
renewable technologies 66
ROSLA (Raising of School Leaving
Age) 99

Samuel Whitbread Academy 33–5
school(s)
boarding 88
BRIT 36–8
career and technical high 40–1
English middle 142–8
'Free' 58
grammar 4–5, 11, 27, 30, 57, 63,
86, 91–4, 119, 122–6
independent see independent
school perspective
middle 6, 17
modern grammar 93
post-war technical 125–6
preparatory 86–8
secondary modern 4, 5, 27, 33,
44, 93, 126–8
senior 65, 87–91
Studio 25, 40, 64, 68
'Schools: Building on Success'
(David Blunkett's green
paper) 2

Science at the Black Country UTC, Walsall 51

secondary education in England 3–7
14 as school leaving age 3
committee on 'The Education of the Adolescent' 4
Education Act (1902) 3
Education Act (1944) 4
middle schools 6
policy of common access 5
policy of comprehensive secondary education 5
Secondary Regulations (1904) 3
selective technical schools 5
technical *see* technical secondary education in England
three-tier system 6

secondary modern schools 4, 5, 27, 33, 44, 93, 126–8

senior school 65, 87–91

sixth-form college 57

Specialist High Skills Majors 112

Spens Report (1938) 120

sports and creative arts pathway 21, 35–8

Studio Schools 25, 40, 64, 68

summer internships 78

technical pathway 21, 27–32, 46, 48, 50, 53

technical secondary education in England
early twentieth century 122–3, 134–6
future 138–40
National Curriculum 133
1930s and 1940s (second rise) 123–5

1960s 128–9
1970s and 1980s 129–31
nineteenth-century origins 119–21
post-war technical schools 125–6
secondary modern schools 126–8
TVEI 131–2
2010 (coalition government) 136–8
vocational qualifications 133–4

tertiary college 57

Thatcher, Margaret 5, 92

transportation 66, 113

unemployment 95–6

Universities and Colleges Admissions Service (UCAS) 95

university technical college (UTC) 27–32
Black Country UTC (case study) 30–2
cross-party support 29
pattern in 20, 22
success, reasons 29–30

Wellcome Trust Centre for Neuroimaging 12

Welsh Baccalaureate 54

Wolf Report on Vocational Education 8, 39, 46, 62, 82, 137

work-based learning 39, 41, 76, 78, 83, 112

work ethos and skills of British youth 95

Working Group on 14–19 Reform 54, 135

W.T. Grant Foundation 71

Young Apprenticeship (YA) 38